Table of Contents

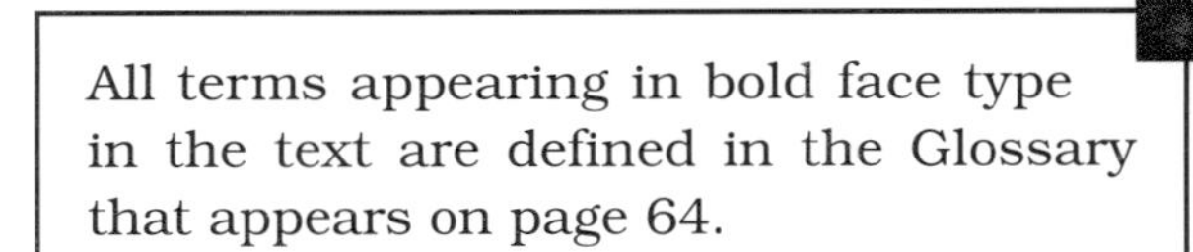
All terms appearing in bold face type in the text are defined in the Glossary that appears on page 64.

1

or as long as anyone can remember, and even longer, **Aboriginal people** have lived in North America. They are the original settlers of the territory we now call Canada. All people tell stories about where they came from. These stories help to explain the world and everyone's place in it.

Some of these stories try to explain the origins of things. They are called creation stories.

Every group of Aboriginal people in Canada has its own creation story. Here is one example, told by the Wendat [WEN-dat] and Haudenosaunee [ha-duh-nuh-SAH-nee] people who live in what is now Ontario and Quebec.

Stories like this one about the woman falling from the sky help to explain how humans are related to other creatures and where they fit into the natural world.

In the beginning, there was nothing but water—nothing but a wide, wide sea. The only people in the world were the animals that live in and on the water.

Then down from the sky world a woman fell, a divine person. Two loons flying over the water happened to look up and see her falling. Quickly they placed themselves beneath her and made a cushion for her to rest upon. Thus they saved her from drowning.

While they held her, they cried with a loud voice to the other animals, asking for their help. As soon as Great Turtle learned the reason for the call, he stepped forth. "Give her to me," he said to the loons. "Put her on my back. My back is broad."

Then the council, discussing what they should do to save the life of the woman, decided that she must have earth to live on. So Great Turtle sent the creatures to dive to the bottom of the sea and bring up some earth.

The woman took the earth and placed it around the edge of Great Turtle's shell. There it became the beginning of dry land. On all sides the land grew larger and larger, until at last it formed a great country. All this country was borne on the back of the Great Turtle, and it is yet today. Great Turtle still bears the earth on his back.

(Story adapted from Ella Elizabeth Clark, Indian Legends of Canada, Toronto, McClelland and Stewart, 1960, 99.1-2)

In The Beginning

Europeans who came to live in Canada developed their own understanding of how humans first came to America. They think that the first people walked across the Bering Strait into America from Siberia. This could have happened during the last Ice Age, when the Bering Strait was dry land.

According to this theory, the first people migrated across America, following the big game animals that were their prey. They settled in different parts of the continent. They practised different customs and spoke different languages. Slowly these first peoples developed into the many Aboriginal groups we know today.

No matter which story you believe, they both agree on an important point: the Aboriginal people lived in America long before anyone else.

An Ice Age was a time many thousands of years ago when the world was much colder than it is today. It was so cold that vast areas of the oceans froze and much of North America was covered by huge sheets of ice. As the world got warmer, and the ice melted, it became possible for people to live in North America.

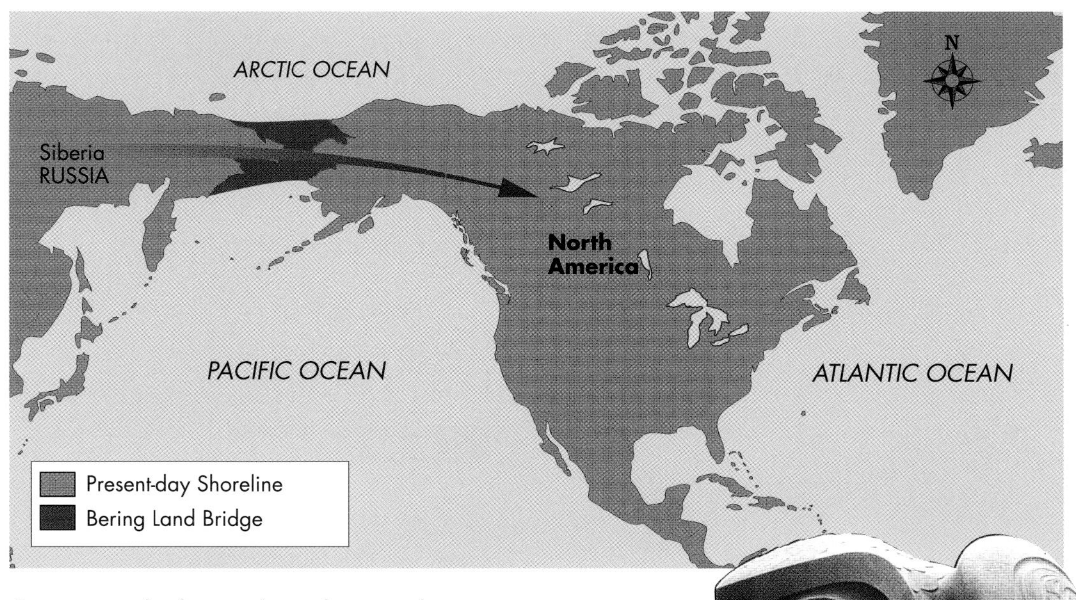

Scientists believe that during the last **Ice Age** *much of the Earth's waters froze, causing the level of the oceans to drop. As a result, a bridge of dry land surfaced between Asia and North America. This area is called Beringia. It may be the route followed by the earliest explorers of America. Later, as the ice melted, the water level in the oceans rose, and Beringia was swallowed up by the sea.*

This huge sculpture by Haida [HY-duh] artist Bill Reid is called The Raven and the First Men. *It illustrates a creation story of the Haida people who live on the Queen Charlotte Islands in British Columbia. This story tells how the original humans emerged from a clam shell.*

SOMETHING TO DO

1. Research a creation story told by another Aboriginal group in Canada. Be a storyteller yourself. Share the story you have researched with your class.
2. Do you have a story explaining how you, your family, or your ancestors arrived in Canada? Suggest reasons why these stories are important.

2

Archaeologists have found artifacts that show people were living in Canada at least 10 500 years ago. These artifacts include stone tools and spear points found buried in the ground at ancient hunting camps in the Yukon, northern British Columbia, and Nova Scotia. The people who made these objects were big game hunters. They tracked down giant bison, moose, caribou, and mountain sheep, killing them with spears. They ate the meat and used the skins to make tents and clothing. They were the distant ancestors of today's Aboriginal peoples.

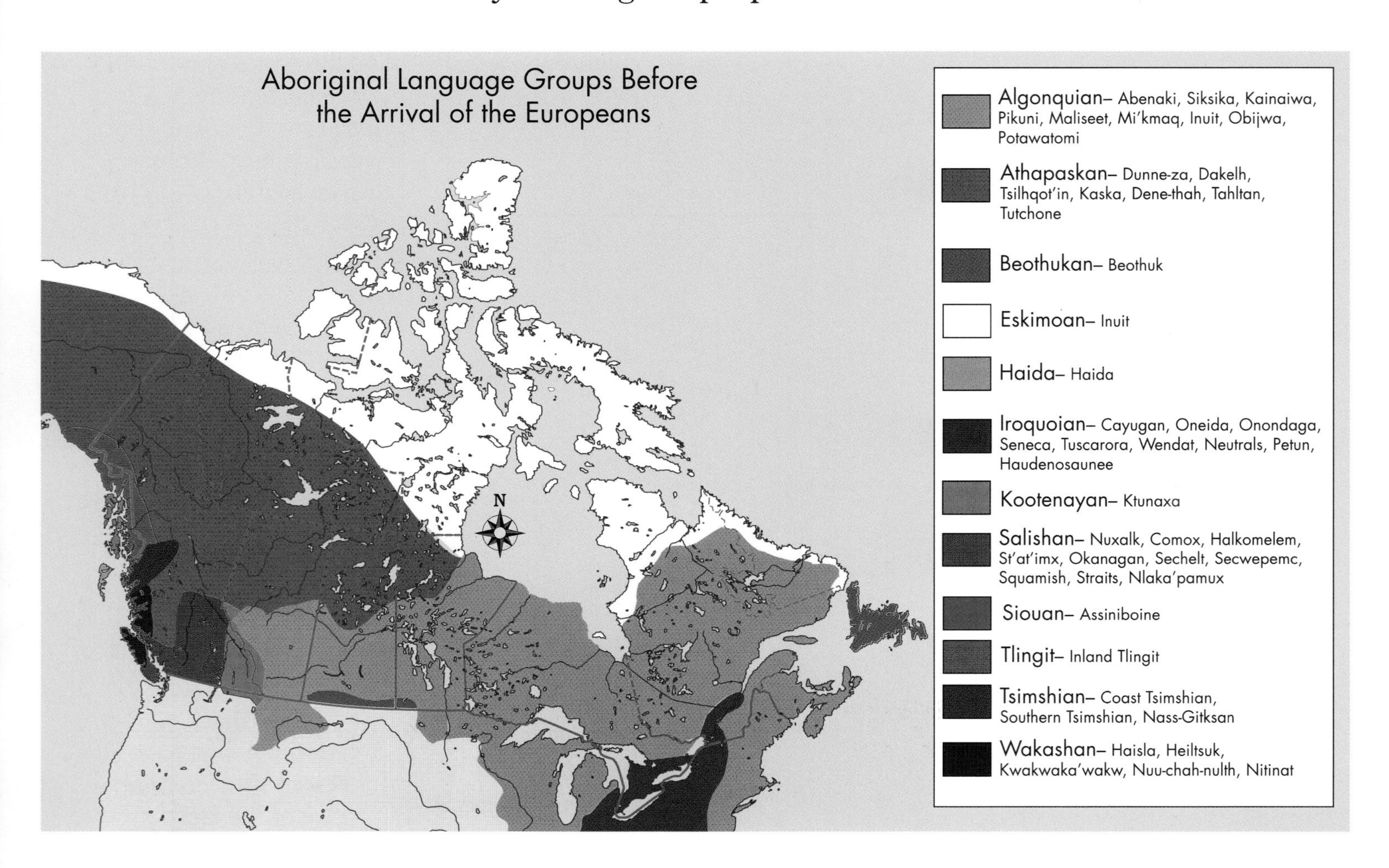

Using an atlas, CD ROMs, or the Internet, briefly describe the landscape and climate of the areas inhabited by the Beothuk, Wendat, Ojibwa (in Northern Ontario), Assiniboine, and the Wakashan group.

As time passed, the Aboriginal peoples moved onto the grassy plains and the valleys of the interior, and to the islands and inlets along the coast. Slowly they developed different languages and different ways of life. Over the years they evolved into the many Aboriginal groups that were present in Canada when the first European explorers arrived.

The Inuit who lived in the Far North learned to make their houses out of snow and hunted seals and polar bears. The groups who lived in the woodlands travelled in small bands looking for wild game. They trapped small animals and camped where fish were plentiful. In the lowlands, where the soil was rich and the climate agreeable, other groups cleared the forest and grew corn. On the coasts, the people relied on fish for food and made canoes to travel across the water.

In each part of Canada, Aboriginal people had a way of life that was based on the land and the resources they found there. Another word for a way of life is **culture**. Culture includes the food that we eat, the clothes we wear, the kind of houses we live in, and the music we listen to. Culture also includes our language, our religion, and the type of **government** we have.

The variety of languages that used to exist in Canada shows how different each group of Aboriginal people was.

There were probably 50 different languages spoken in Canada when the first European explorers arrived. In British Columbia, where high mountains kept the groups separate from each other, there were as many as 24 languages spoken. Some of these languages have disappeared, but many continue to be spoken by different Aboriginal groups. They are the oldest languages in Canada.

Archaeology is the science of digging up the past. By studying the remains of houses, tools and other **artifacts**, archaeologists learn about events that took place in the past and the people who lived long ago.

These artifacts are evidence used by archaeologists to prove that people were living in the territory we now call Canada over 10 000 years ago. Visit a local museum to see if any such artifacts were found near your community.

SOMETHING TO DO

1. Make a chart like this one.

Region	Food	Clothing	Travel
Far North			
Woodlands			
Plains			
Pacific Coast			
Atlantic Coast			

a) Think about what you know about the climate and landscape in the different parts of Canada. How do you think the Aboriginal people who lived there found food? What did they do for clothing, and how did they travel? Put your findings into the chart.

b) If you had a choice, which part of Canada would you prefer to live in if you were an Aboriginal person? Why?

2. It is many years in the future. Your own home and everything in it has been buried by time. An archaeologist has now dug up your house. What things will have survived over the years? What would the archaeologist learn about your way of life?

3

he Pacific Coast of Canada is a region of mild climate and lush forests. Warm air blows in off the ocean, and as it rises over the mountains, it drops its load of moisture as rain. As a result, the coast of what we know as British Columbia is one of the wettest spots on Earth. All the rain produces a rain forest, where trees grow as tall as 25-storey buildings.

A large village had as many as a dozen houses, called longhouses, or bighouses. Several related families lived in a single house.

The rain forest provided the Aboriginal people who lived on the coast with everything they needed to live. They built large houses made from planks cut from the trees. They used the trunks of the trees to make canoes, and bark and roots to weave clothing, mats, fish nets, rope, and baskets. Today the people still use wood to carve the totem poles and masks that are such an important part of their culture.

On the coast, people lived by fishing, collecting shellfish and hunting seals and sea lions. During the winter they lived in large villages of many houses. When better weather came in the spring, they moved to smaller camps to gather food. The most important fish was the salmon, which returned to the coast every summer. The people caught enough salmon to last them all year. They preserved the fish by drying it in the sun or smoking it over fires.

Another favourite fish was the silvery eulachon. Each spring eulachon swarmed in huge numbers at the mouths of the rivers. They were a very greasy fish. When dried, they burned like a candle. The coastal people traded the oil from the eulachon to other groups living further inland.

Because resources were plentiful on the coast, life was easier there than in other parts of the country.

People of the Coast

The people of the coast were sea-going people. Their villages were always at the water's edge. They had no roads or wheeled vehicles, but travelled everywhere by water in their log canoes. These canoes were beautifully shaped, polished, and decorated with designs and carvings. They were works of art, made by trained artists.

The people had more time to take part in ceremonies and make works of art. One of the most important ceremonies was the potlatch. Potlatches were held to celebrate special moments in the life of the community. They were held to honour someone who had died, or to celebrate a wedding, or to name a new chief. Potlatches were held for many different reasons.

A potlatch might last several days, even weeks. There was feasting and dancing and people giving speeches. Guests received presents to thank them for being witness to the event. They returned to their own communities and told everyone what had taken place. In this way, a potlatch was an important way of keeping a record of events.

When Europeans arrived on the coast, they did not understand how important the potlatch was for the Aboriginal people there. They wanted the Aboriginal people to give up their traditions, and so they passed a law making the potlatch illegal. It remained against the law for many years. However, since 1951 the potlatch has been legal again. It remains an important ceremony for some Aboriginal people in British Columbia today.

Totem poles are tall pillars of carved wood that stand in a village. They are made by skilled carvers from a single cedar tree. Totem poles show figures from history and legend, and important crests and designs from the owner's family. They are still a familiar sight in British Columbia.

SOMETHING TO DO

1. Why do you think the villages of the coastal people were located near water? Think about where your own community is located. Can you suggest why it is located where it is?
2. Study the photograph of the canoe and make a drawing or model of your own canoe. Decorate its bow with colourful designs. Why would the coastal people have needed a canoe like this?
3. Describe how the peoples of the West Coast used cedar trees to meet their needs. Answer in chart form, using the headings: transportation, shelter/clothing, artwork, food/household items.

4

Crouching low in his hiding place, the teenage boy watched as a dark cloud of dust came closer and closer. At first he could see tiny specks in the distance. Then the specks grew larger and became a stampeding herd of animals. When the thundering herd was almost upon him, he jumped up, waving his arms and shouting. The animals veered away and ran toward a high cliff. Over the animals tumbled, falling to their deaths on the rocks below.

These bones, found at the base of the Head-Smashed-In buffalo jump in Southern Alberta, are over 5700 years old.

At one time, the flat, grassy plains that cover the interior of North America teemed with herds of buffalo. Their thundering stampede could be heard for many kilometres. The early explorers reported that herds covered the prairie as far as the eye could see.

The buffalo was an important animal for the Aboriginal peoples of the Plains. It provided meat to eat, hides to make clothing, bones to make tools and weapons, and sinew to make thread. One way the people hunted the buffalo was to frighten them into stampeding over cliffs.

The Plains people were **nomadic**. They followed the herds of buffalo from place to place. They lived in cone-shaped tents made of buffalo hides, called **tipis**.

Horses were brought to North America by the earliest Europeans. When the horse arrived on the plains, it made a big difference in the life of the people. The horse made it easier for the buffalo hunters to move about in search of the herds. They still hunted the buffalo in the old way, by driving the animals over a cliff, but they also chased them on horseback, shooting them with bows and arrows.

With the arrival of European settlers on the plains, the buffalo

People of the Buffalo

Tipis were made of a circle of poles covered by buffalo skins. A hole in the roof allowed smoke from the fire to escape. The door was a flap of leather. Tipis could be folded up and carried from place to place.

began to disappear. The newcomers built railways that divided the great herds and made it hard for them to move with the seasons. Hunters came into the country to kill the buffalo for sport. These hunters only wanted the tongues of the animals, or their furry hides to make coats. The rest of the animal was left to rot in the sun. In a short time the vast herds of buffalo had disappeared.

THE VISION QUEST

Like other Aboriginal groups, the Plains people believed in mysterious forces, or spirits, which guided the world. Their lives depended on understanding these forces and sharing in their power. Every living thing had a spirit with thoughts and feelings. The people tried to please the spirits by offering them gifts and not offending them.

In their youth, Aboriginal people tried to make contact with a spirit. It was a coming-of-age ritual, known as a vision quest. The young person went off alone for many days of fasting and prayer. At length, a spirit animal might appear, as if in a dream. The animal shared special songs and prayers and showed the young person what objects would be sacred for the rest of his or her life. That animal would always remain sacred to the person who had seen it.

Some people were closer to the spirits than others. They seemed to be able to call on the spirits on behalf of all the people for guidance. Sometimes they could even use their power to look into the future. These people with special powers were called **shamans**. They were the religious leaders of the people.

DID YOU KNOW?

The buffalo hunters made a dish called **pemmican**. They dried the meat, pounded it into a powder and mixed it with fat and berries to make a very healthy food. When fur traders came onto the Plains, they relied on pemmican for a large part of their diet.

SOMETHING TO DO

1. How did the Plains people use the resources in their natural environment to obtain food?
2. Do some research to find out what changes the horse brought to the Plains people. Write down all the ideas you have. Then share your ideas with the rest of the class to come up with a complete list.
3. Do some research using books, the Internet, or CD ROMs to describe the trees, plants, and animals (other than the buffalo) that lived on the prairies. Were any of these used by the Plains people? How?

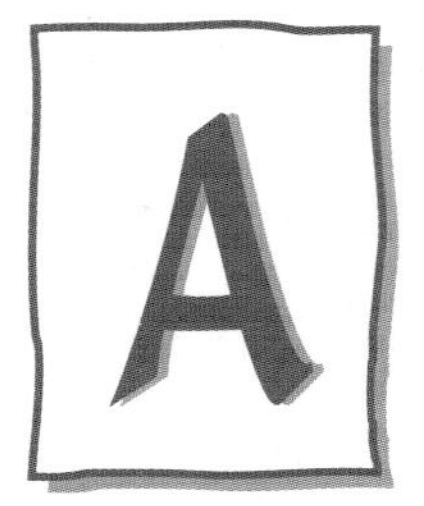

ll the **First Nations** people of Canada were hunters and fishers. They survived by hunting and trapping animals, catching fish and gathering wild plants. However, the Iroquoian people who lived around the southern Great Lakes and in the valley of the St. Lawrence River also used another method to obtain food. These people were Canada's original farmers.

The Iroquoian people consisted of several different groups. The Wendat, the Petun and the Neutrals lived in what we now call southern Ontario, between Lake Huron and Lake Ontario. The Haudenosaunee, called the Iroquois by the Europeans, lived south of Lake Ontario in what is now New York State. Later in history, some Haudenosaunee moved north into Ontario and Quebec where they live today.

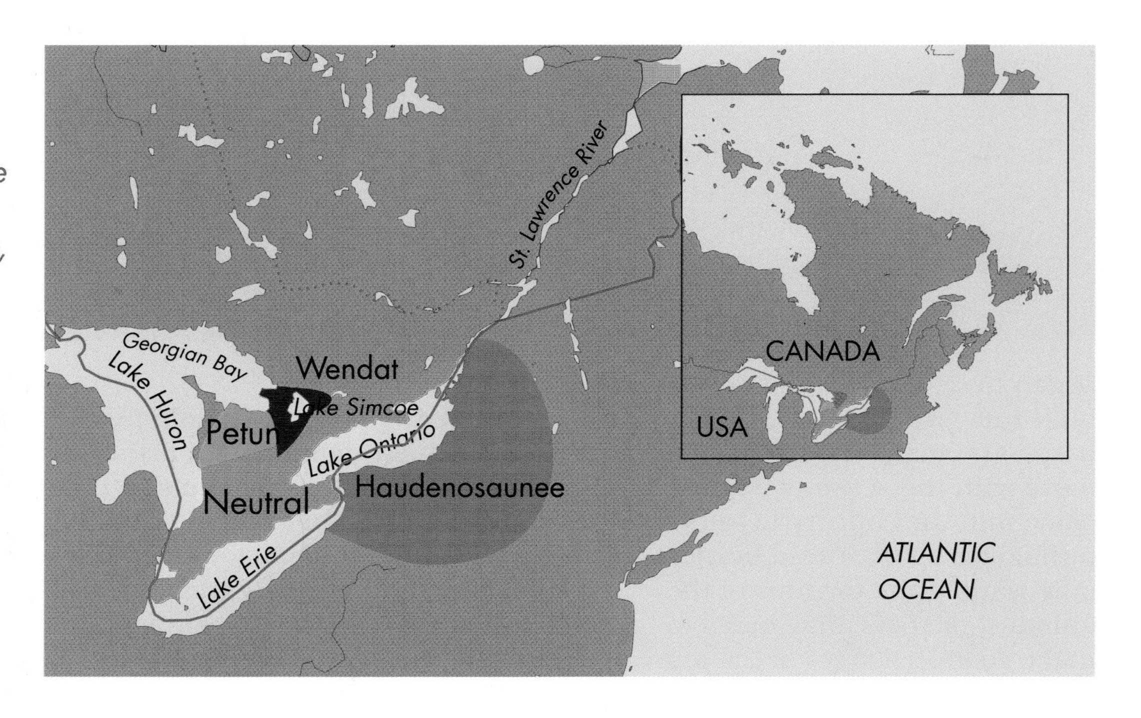

DID YOU KNOW?

The name of our country, Canada, comes from an Iroquoian word, *Kanata*, which may mean "hamlet" or "village."

THE IROQUOIANS

The Iroquoians consisted of several different nations. They were considered to be related because they spoke a similar language, but each nation had its own customs.

The Wendat (called the Huron by the Europeans) were one Iroquoian nation. They lived between Lake Ontario and Lake Huron in an area known as Huronia. They lived in about 20 large villages. Each village was surrounded by a log stockade, or wall, to protect the villagers from attacks by their enemies. Their neighbours were the Petuns and the Neutrals, two other Iroquoian groups who lived in similar villages.

Each village consisted of many lodges, called **longhouses**, which were made of sheets of bark covering a frame of poles. Each longhouse contained several families, totalling as many as 100 people. An aisle ran down the middle of the longhouse where each family had its cooking fire. Against the wall, each family had its own living quarters, with sleeping platforms and storage areas. The first Europeans who visited them found the longhouses crowded, smoky, and noisy. But for the Iroquoians, they were comfortable, lively centres of family life.

Women had special influence in Iroquoian society. The head of each longhouse was a respected older woman, or matron. It was the matrons who chose the chiefs, arranged marriages and made other important decisions.

The people belonged to different groups called **clans**. All the members of a clan thought of themselves as relatives. Each clan was symbolized by an animal—a bear, a wolf, a turtle, or some other animal. Members of a clan did not marry each other, but married members of a different clan.

Clans met together to make important political decisions.

Beyond the walls of the village were the fields where the Iroquoians grew crops. Their main crop was corn, a plant that did not yet exist in Europe. In fact, the Iroquoians were making popcorn, and even candy corn (dipped in maple syrup) long before the Europeans had ever tasted it. They also grew beans, squash, and melons. The Petuns were known particularly for growing tobacco.

In the spring the people cleared the land by cutting the trees and burning them. Using tools made of moose antlers, they worked the soil and planted the seeds. All summer the women tended the crops, chasing away birds and rodents and pulling the weeds. September was harvest time when the leaves on the trees turned bright colours and the corn was ready to be picked and dried.

The Iroquoians divided the work between men and women. Women did almost all the work of growing the crops. The men fished, hunted and went on trips to trade with neighbouring groups.

THE ALGONQUIANS

In the woodlands to the north of the Iroquoian people lived several other groups known as the Algonquians [al-GONG-kwuns]. The Algonquians spoke a different language than the Iroquoians and followed a different way of life. Their country was dense forest land, broken by many rivers and lakes. The Algonqians did grow some food, but their country was not well-suited to farming. It did contain a wealth of animal life, however. Deer, bear, moose, rabbit and beaver are just some of the wildlife that live in the woodlands, along with lots of fish and many types of berries and nuts.

Iroquoian villages were located close to the fields and to streams with clean water. The village might hold 800 to 1000 people. Each village was connected by trails, and runners carried news and announcements from village to village. Every decade or so the village had to move because the soil was no longer good for farming and the wood supply was used up.

DID YOU KNOW?

Lacrosse is Canada's national game. It was invented by the Haudenosaunee, who believed that playing it gave them the skills to be great warriors.

The Obijwa word for wild rice is mamomin. *This name comes from the word* Manitou, *meaning Great Spirit, and* meenun, *meaning delicacy. It is a very nutritional grain that is high in vitamins and minerals, and low in fat.*

Wild rice was one of the plants harvested by the Algonquian people, especially by the Ojibwa. Wild rice grows in marshy areas at the edge of lakes. When the plants were ripe, harvesters went among them in their canoes. They bent the tall stalks and beat them with paddles, knocking the kernels of rice into the bottom of the canoe. The people also tapped the trunks of maple trees to draw off the sap for making maple syrup.

The Algonquians did not live in large, fortified villages as the Iroquoians did. For much of the year they lived in small family groups, camping in the woods as they followed the animals they hunted for food. Their homes were cone-shaped lodges made of a frame of young saplings covered with bark or animal skins.

Bark was also used by the Algonquians to build their canoes. Birch bark was preferred because it was light and strong. The bark was stripped from the tree trunks in large sheets, wrapped around a wooden frame and sewn together with roots to make a canoe. When the waterways froze in winter, the people moved about on snowshoes, pulling their belongings on **toboggans**.

At maple sugar time, or when the wild rice harvest began, the people came together in larger groups. This was a time for socializing, when news was exchanged and spiritual ceremonies were carried out. There was dancing, feasting and games.

The Algonquians hunted large animals such as moose and deer, using spears and bows and arrows. Smaller animals, such as rabbits, were caught in snares and traps. The people also relied on fish from the rivers and lakes, caught using nets, spears, or hooks made of bone. Whenever the hunt was successful, the food was shared among all the members of the group.

Algonquian and Iroquoian groups traded extensively. As farmers and hunters, they had much to offer one another. The Algonquians had meat, fish, furs, wild rice and bark canoes. The Iroquoians had tobacco, corn, and other crops. Trading parties travelled great distances across Ontario, using the rivers and well-worn trails that criss-crossed the territory. Trade was more than just an exchange of goods. It was also a time to renew friendships, to feast and dance, and to exchange gifts.

The Algonquians also lived in what we now call Ontario. There were several Algonquian groups, including the Algonquins, the Nipissings, the Ottawa and the Ojibwa. Their territories ranged from the Ottawa Valley west across Ontario to Lake Superior.

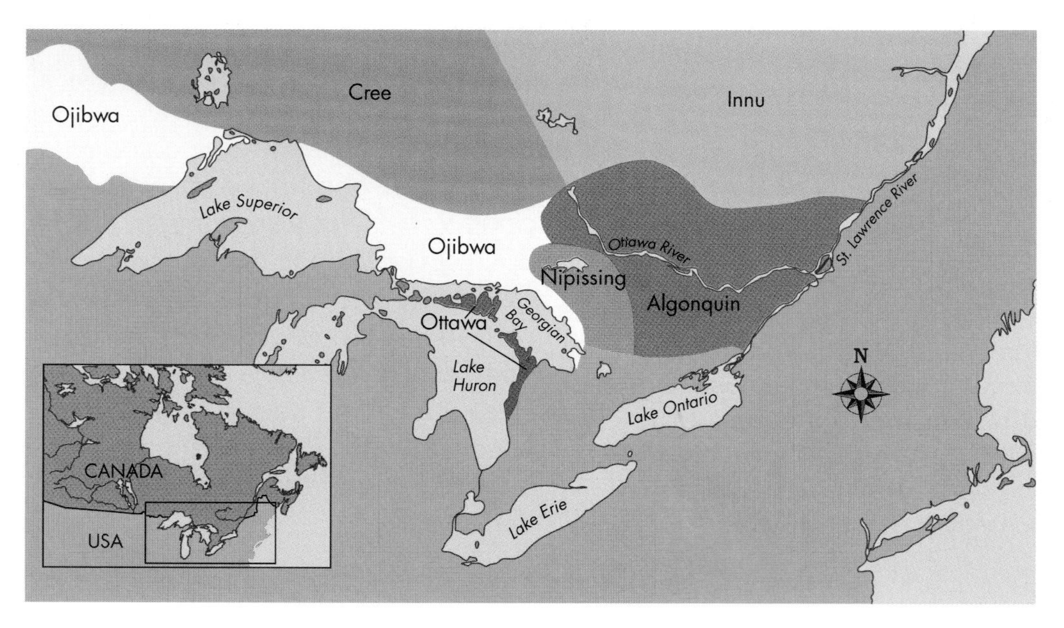

This painting, done in 1880, is called Encampment of Woodland Indians. *It was painted by the artist Thomas Mower Martin. It shows the bark lodges and canoes of the Algonquian people.*

Sometimes the friendly trade relations turned sour and the groups sent parties of warriors to raid each other's villages. This was not warfare as we know it today, with armies trying to conquer the territory of an enemy. Raiding consisted of small groups of just a few warriors who wanted to prove their courage in battle or to take revenge because a member of their family had been killed.

Later, after the arrival of Europeans, raiding became more deadly. Aboriginal groups fought to gain control the fur trade with the Europeans. In the 1640s, for example, the Haudenosaunee came north in Ontario and almost completely wiped out the Wendat villages there. This warfare over the fur trade caused much disruption among the Aboriginal groups and a movement of some peoples into new territories.

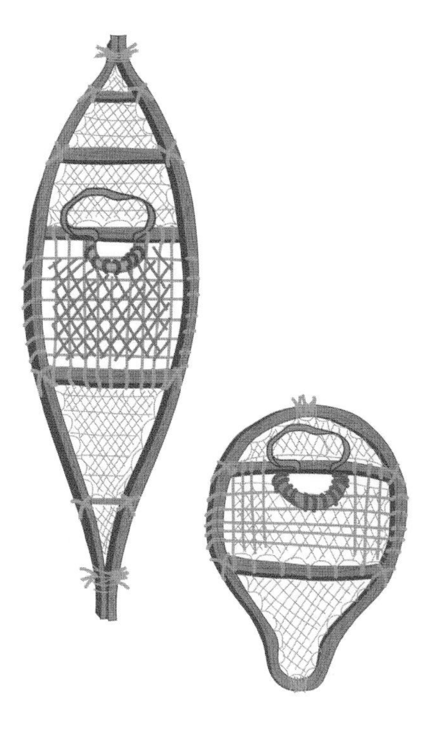

Hunting and travelling also took place in the winter, so Aboriginal people wore snowshoes that made it easy to walk on deep snow. They were made of leather thongs woven across a wood frame.

SOMETHING TO DO

1. What do you think the major difference in lifestyle was between hunting people and people who grew their own food in addition to hunting?
2. Would you like to live in an Iroquoian village? Write down three reasons for your answer.
3. Aboriginal people have made important contributions to Canada. Using a chart like the one below, list the contributions made by Iroquoian and Algonquian groups.

Iroquoian		Algonquian
	transportation	
	shelter	
	clothing	
	exploration	
	food	

he Mi'kmaq (MIG-mah) lived along the seacoast and rivers of what we now call the Atlantic provinces. Animals and fish were plentiful in their territory, and the Mi'kmaq relied on hunting and fishing to survive.

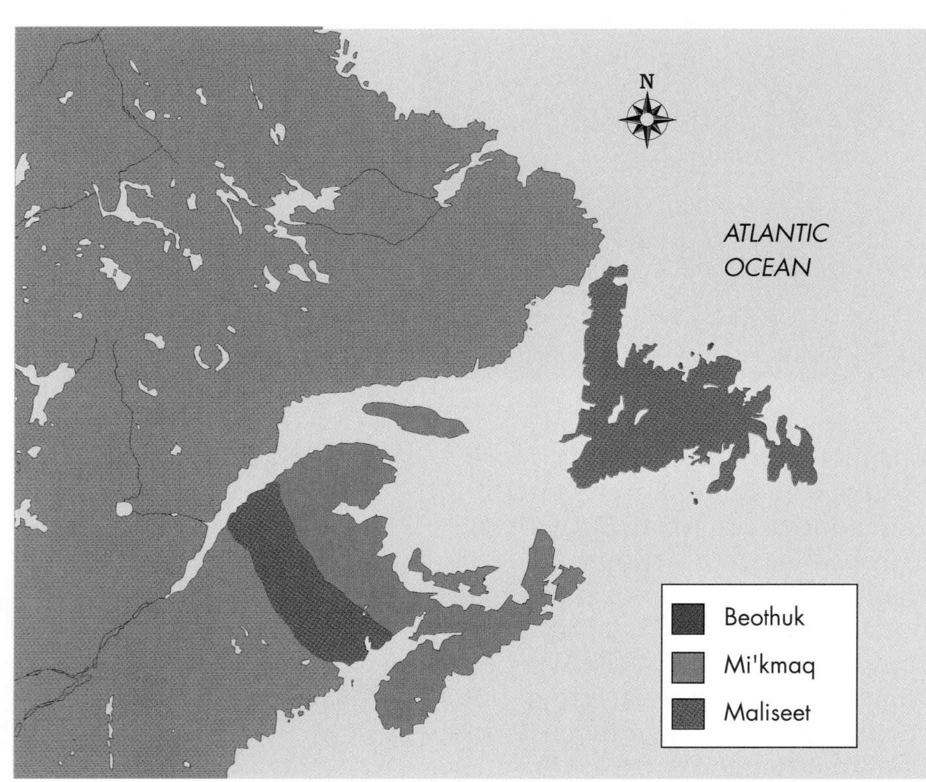

This map shows the main Aboriginal groups in Atlantic Canada.

Moose, caribou, beaver, and birds: all these animals were part of the diet of the Mi'kmaq. They also gathered berries and nuts in the forest. In the summer they turned their attention to the sea. Along the shore they collected shellfish and hunted seals and giant walruses. Along with food, these animals also provided the Mi'kmaq with skins to make clothing, and bones to make tools.

The Mi'kmaq were skilled fishers. Often they fished at night by canoe. While one person paddled, another stood in the bow holding a torch of burning bark. Attracted by the bright light, the fish swam near. The fisher struck suddenly with a spear, then wrestled the thrashing fish into the canoe.

The Mi'kmaq lived in **wigwams**, shelters made of tree bark or animal skins supported by a frame of poles. These dwellings had doors, but no windows. Smoke from the fires escaped through a hole in the roof. The Mi'kmaq also used the bark of the birch tree to make their canoes.

Like all Aboriginal groups that relied on hunting for survival, the Mi'kmaq had a close relationship with the world of nature. To the Mi'kmaq, animals were beings just like themselves. Every animal had a spirit that deserved respect. The Mi'kmaq believed that animals allowed themselves to be killed so that people would have food. The Mi'kmaq used many rituals and ceremonies to try to influence the way the animals behaved during the hunt.

Young Mi'kmaq did not go to school as children do today. They learned by watching and listening. They watched their families go about their daily chores and as they grew older they began to take part. Young girls learned to prepare skins and weave baskets. Young boys learned to trap and hunt. The youngsters listened to the **Elders** tell stories and learned about the history and customs of their people.

Around the year 1500, fishers from Europe began crossing the Atlantic Ocean to fish for cod off the coast of North America. Sometimes the fishers landed on the rocky coast to take on fresh water or cut wood. When they did, they met the Mi'kmaq and began trading with them. The Mi'kmaq were the first people to enter into the fur trade with Europeans.

Another group of Aboriginal peoples on the Atlantic coast were the Beothuks [BEE-aw-thuks]. They lived on the island of

DID YOU KNOW?

For a long time the Mi'kmaq were known as the Micmac because that was the way Europeans pronounced their name. Only recently have the people asked to be called by the name they call themselves.

The East Coast Mi'kmaq

The Mi'kmaq are famous for their baskets made with the quills of porcupine.

Newfoundland. When Europeans arrived, the Beothuks came into conflict with them over the use of food and land. Not having guns, the Beothuks were powerless. They withdrew from the coast to the interior of the island. One by one they died from disease, starvation, and killings until by 1830 there were no Beothuks left alive. An entire people had died away.

This painting of a Mi'kmaq camp was made by an unknown artist about 1850.

SOMETHING TO DO

1. Study the painting of the Mi'kmaq camp. Find examples of the following: shelter, weapons, clothing, transportation. Which things in the painting do you think the Mi'kmaq were using before the arrival of Europeans? Which things do you think they traded from the newcomers? Which things in the painting did Europeans borrow from the Mi'kmaq?
2. Using bark and sticks, or whatever other materials that are available, make a model of a wigwam. What were the advantages of this kind of housing for the Mi'kmaq people? What were the similarities and differences between Mi'kmaq wigwams and the tipis of the Plains people?
3. Do elderly people have a special role in your community? What is it? If not, do you think they should have? Why?

DID YOU KNOW?

Elders are respected by First Nations people for their knowledge and experience. They help to educate children and act as advisors for the group. They have an honoured place in First Nations society.

7

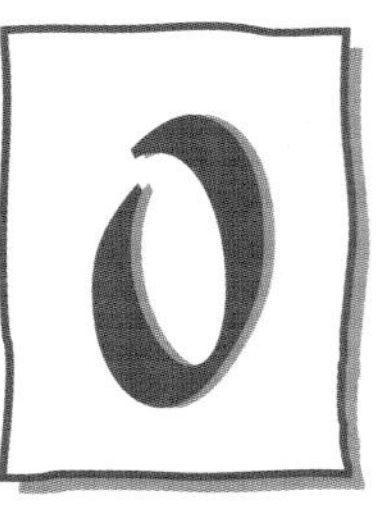

ne thousand years ago the first Europeans came to North America. They were the Vikings. They landed their ships on the rocky coast of what we now call Newfoundland, in a harbour called L'Anse aux Meadows.

This is the type of boat in which the Vikings sailed across the Atlantic. The boats were small by today's standards. They were only about 20 metres long, and open to the wind and storm. Sailors slept on deck and took their meals out in the open, in a climate where it was cold enough for icebergs to form. The boats were powered by a single sail, or by oars. How tiring it must have been to row across the open ocean!

The Vikings were a sea-going people from Norway in northern Europe. Setting out to explore the northern stretches of the Atlantic Ocean, they sailed from island to island until they came to Greenland, where they started a colony.

In 986 a sailor named Bjarni got lost on his way to Greenland. He and his crew drifted in a fog for many days. When the fog lifted Bjarni saw a strange land that he knew was not Greenland. This may have been the first sighting of North America by a European.

Bjarni found his way back home, but a few years later another Viking named Leif Ericsson set out to find the new land. He put ashore at a place he called Vinland, "Land of Wine," referring to wild grapes growing in the area. Leif and his crew put up a small settlement of houses where they built and repaired boats and cut timber to be shipped to Greenland.

One of the people who came to live in Vinland was a woman named Gudrid. She gave birth to a baby boy named Snorre. As far as anyone knows, Snorre was the first non-Aboriginal born in America.

The Vikings met some Aboriginal people who they called "Skraelings." They were probably the ancestors of the Beothuk and Mi'kmaq peoples. The two groups met and traded. But a later meeting ended in a battle in which Vikings and Aboriginal people died. Afraid of another attack, the Vikings left their tiny settlement, never to return.

Sailors of the North Sea

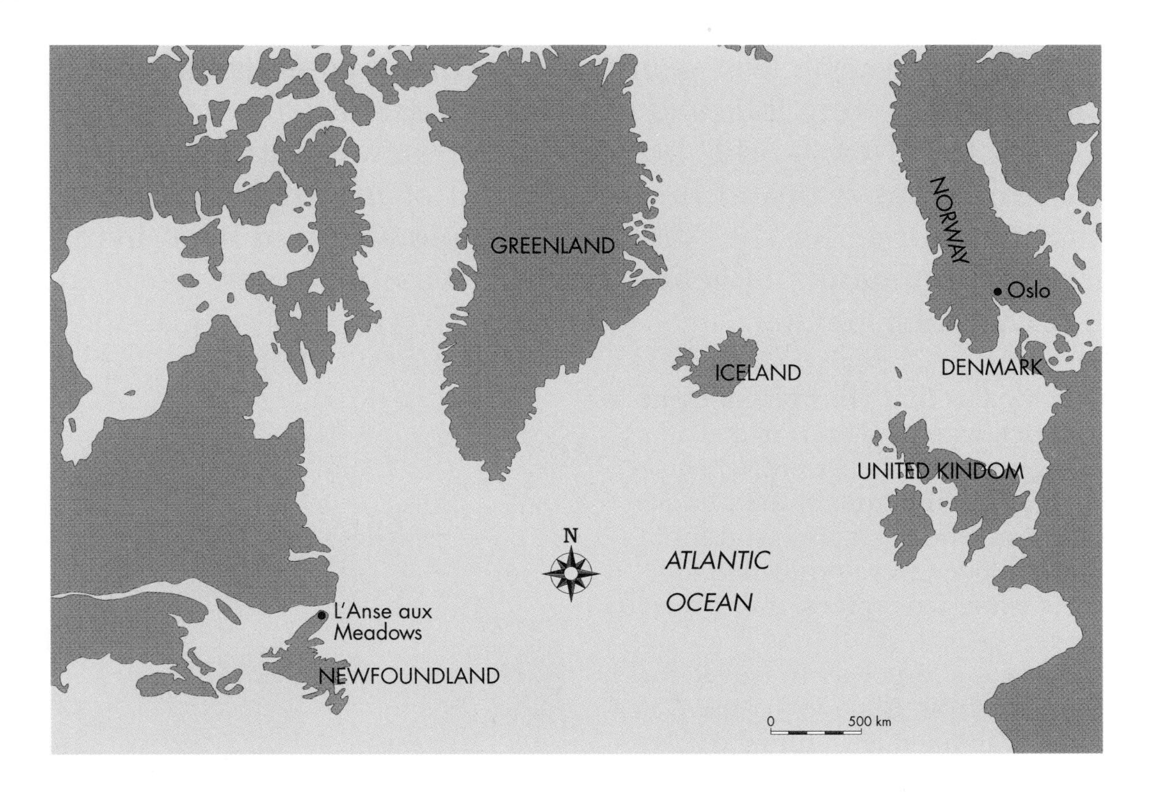

This map shows the North Atlantic area. Greenland is the largest island in the world. Today it is part of Denmark.

DID YOU KNOW?

World Heritage Sites are named by the United Nations. They are special places in the history of the world.

The Vikings told about their voyages in stories called **sagas**. For many hundreds of years, it was not known where the places named in the sagas actually were. In 1960 two Norwegians, Helge and Anne Ingstad, found some ruins at L'Anse aux Meadows on the north coast of Newfoundland. Was this the Vinland of Leif Ericsson? We cannot know for sure. What is known is that these are the remains of a Viking settlement that is 1000 years old. Today the meadow is a National Historic Site, the place where Aboriginal people and Europeans probably met for the first time.

The settlement at L'Anse aux Meadows contained three large houses. Each house had a workshop and a simple furnace for working with metal. In 1978 L'Anse aux Meadows was declared a **World Heritage Site.**

SOMETHING TO DO

1. Trace the map above onto a piece of paper. Draw lines with arrows to show the route Leif Ericsson could have taken from Europe to North America.
2. What materials did the Vikings use to build their dwellings?
3. In groups of four, brainstorm reasons why people such as the Vikings wanted to make settlements in North America. Make a list of the four most important reasons.
4. What concerns do you think the Aboriginal people had about the arrival of strangers in their land? Role-play a speech that an Aboriginal leader might have given to the Vikings as they stepped from their boats.

The Vikings were the first people from Europe to arrive in North America. They were followed by many others. Europeans called America the "New World" because they knew so little about it. To them it was a brand new place, full of mystery and possibility. Of course, for the Aboriginal people who had been living there for thousands of years, America was not a new world at all. It was their home.

One reason that Europeans came to America was in search of a sea-going route to the Orient. The Orient was the area of Asia known today as China, Japan, and India. These places were renowned for their silks, tea, spices, and precious gems.

It was a long way to travel overland from Europe to Asia. The route was filled with many dangers and controlled by traders who charged high prices for the goods. Europeans wanted to find a faster, cheaper route by sailing west across the Atlantic Ocean.

The first European to reach America after the Vikings was Christopher Columbus. Columbus

This map shows the routes followed by traders between Europe and Asia. With your finger, trace the water route the traders hoped they could use to reach Asia. What advantage would an ocean route have had for the Europeans?

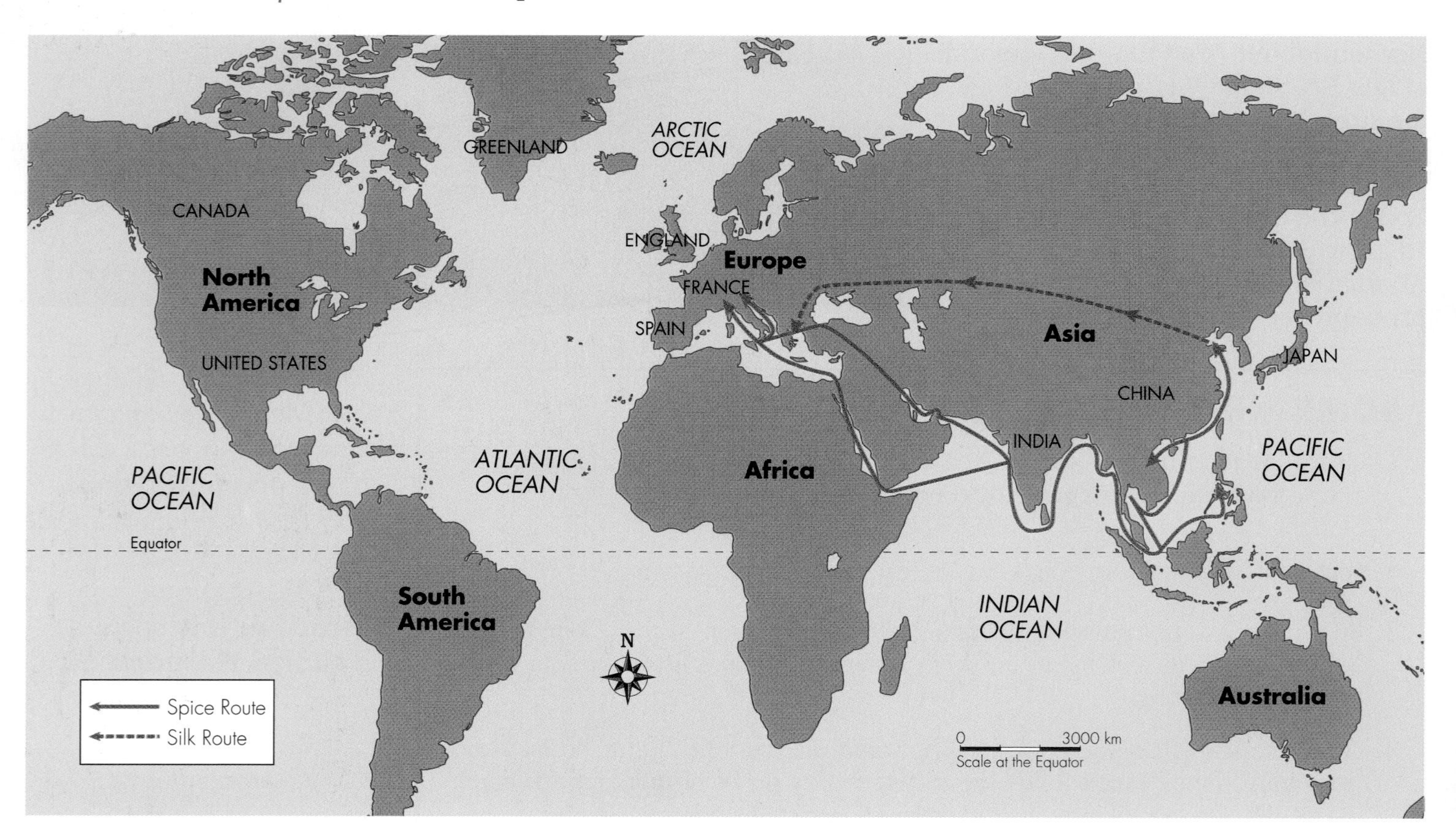

was an Italian sailor working for the King and Queen of Spain. In 1492, he led a group of three sailing ships to find a way across the Atlantic to Asia.

The group arrived at islands known today as the Bahamas. Columbus thought he had arrived in India, however, so he called the Aboriginal people he met there Indians. In fact, he had arrived in the Caribbean and the people were the Arawaks.

Excited by news of Columbus's voyage, several other European countries sent off ships of their own. One of these ships was commanded by John Cabot, who sailed from England across the Atlantic in 1497. We do not know for sure where he went, but Cabot probably landed on Newfoundland or Cape Breton Island. When he returned to Europe, he told of the large number of fish he had seen.

Thanks to the voyages of Columbus, Cabot, and many others, Europeans realized that they had not found a route to Asia. They had to admit that another continent, North America, lay between Europe and Asia. Voyagers continued to try to find a way around the continent to Asia. They called this the **Northwest Passage**.

But at the same time, Europeans began to realize that North America had rich resources of its own. Fishers came to catch the plentiful cod. Traders came to barter for animal furs with the Aboriginal peoples. Not all the contacts were peaceful. Rumors of gold and other precious metals had the Europeans dreaming of fabulous riches. In the case of Columbus and the Spanish, they enslaved the Arawaks and killed many thousands of them in their desperate search for gold.

Along with the explorers came **missionaries**, who journeyed to America to spread their spiritual beliefs. Europeans were deeply religious. They believed that Christianity was the only true religion and that it was their duty to introduce it to every corner of the world. Europeans did not understand that the Aboriginal peoples had spiritual beliefs of their own. They were determined to bring Christianity to North America.

SOMETHING TO DO

1. List three reasons why Europeans wanted to explore North America.
2. Here are the names of four other early explorers of the coast of North America: Martin Frobisher, Giovanni de Verrazzano, Henry Hudson, William Baffin. Choose one and do some research into his life. You can begin by looking at the timeline on page 25. Include a map with your findings to show where your explorer went. Try to answer these four questions.
   - When did your explorer come to America?
   - What was your explorer looking for?
   - Where did your explorer travel?
   - What new area(s) did your explorer add to the map of the North America?
3. Today we are exploring in outer space by sending astronauts to the moon and beyond. Europeans had their reasons for exploring North America. What reasons do humans have to explore in space?

DID YOU KNOW?

Christopher Columbus made a total of four voyages across the Atlantic Ocean. He believed to his death that he had reached Asia.

9

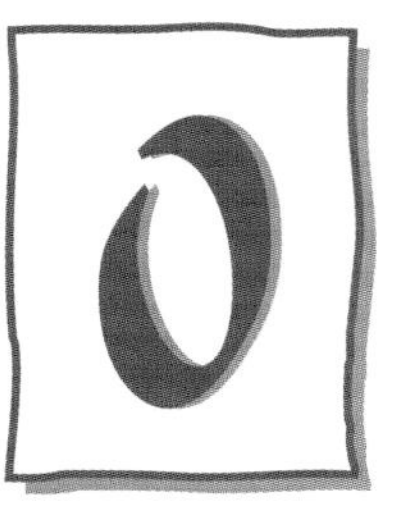

On a day in July, 1534, a large group of Mi'kmaq people paddled their canoes along the shore of the Bay of Chaleur. Suddenly the people came upon a rowboat filled with strange-looking men who spoke a language the Mi'kmaq did not understand.

The leader of the strangers, a French sea captain named Jacques Cartier, wrote about what happened next. "A great number of these people leaped ashore with a great shout. [They] made signs to us to land, holding up skins on the ends of sticks."

Cartier and his men were a little frightened and retreated to their sailing ship nearby. But the next day the French and the Mi'kmaq met again. "We made signs to them that we wished them no harm," Cartier wrote, "and in sign of this two of our men landed to approach them, and bring them knives and other ironware, with a red hat to give to their chief.

"They gave us all they had, keeping nothing back; and were compelled to go away stark naked, making signs to us that they would return the next day with more skins."

The actions of the Mi'kmaq suggest that they already knew how to trade with Europeans. But the events described by Cartier are the first written record of trade between Europeans and Aboriginal people in Canada.

Jacques Cartier had been sent to North America by the King of France with orders to find a water route to China. He sailed around the northern tip of Newfoundland and across the Gulf of St. Lawrence. A few days after meeting the Mi'kmaq in the Bay of Chaleur he landed again and raised a cross, claiming the land for France.

Another group of Aboriginal people were witness to this event.

There was no portrait of Cartier made during his lifetime. This artist was imagining what Cartier might have looked like.

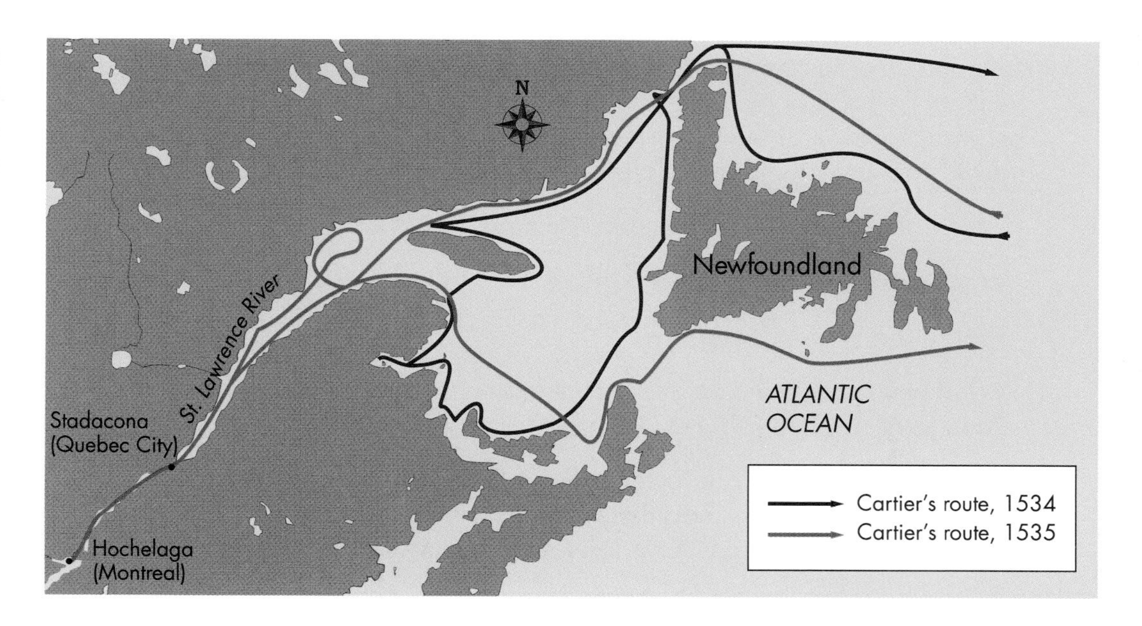

This map shows the route followed by Jacques Cartier on his first two trips to the St. Lawrence River.

They were the Haudenosaunee from inland who had come to the coast to fish. Donnacona, a Haudenosaunee leader, protested that the land did not belong to the French. But Cartier did not listen. Instead, he took Donnacona's two sons back to France as evidence of what he had found.

A year later, in 1535, Cartier returned to America with three ships and 110 men. He brought the two Haudenosaunee men with him. They were called Domagaya and Taignoagny. They led Cartier to the mouth of the St. Lawrence River. His ships sailed up the river to the village of Stadacona where Donnacona's people lived. Here the French built a small fort and spent the winter.

The French were not prepared for the cold. They took sick and many of them died before Cartier learned from the Haudenosaunee how to boil cedar to make medicine. This was just one of many things the Aboriginal people taught the Europeans about survival. In the spring the survivors sailed back to France, this time kidnapping Donnacona himself, as well as nine other villagers.

It was six years before Cartier returned. During that time in Europe, Donnacona and all but one of the other Haudenosaunee captives died of European diseases. Because Donnacona had not come back with Cartier, the Haudenosaunee became unfriendly. After suffering another terrible winter near Stadacona, the French dug up some "gold" and sailed for home. The gold turned out to be pyrite, a worthless mineral also known as "fool's gold," and a small settlement they had left behind turned out to be a failure. For the time being, at least, Canada did not seem like a place that offered anything to people from Europe.

DID YOU KNOW?

Cartier and his men suffered from scurvy, a disease caused by a lack of vitamin C. The needles and bark of the white cedar contain vitamin C. It was many years before Europeans understood how to cure scurvy.

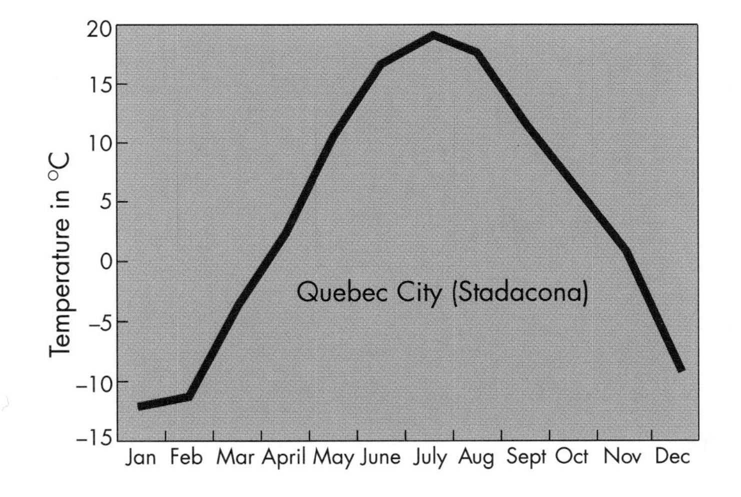

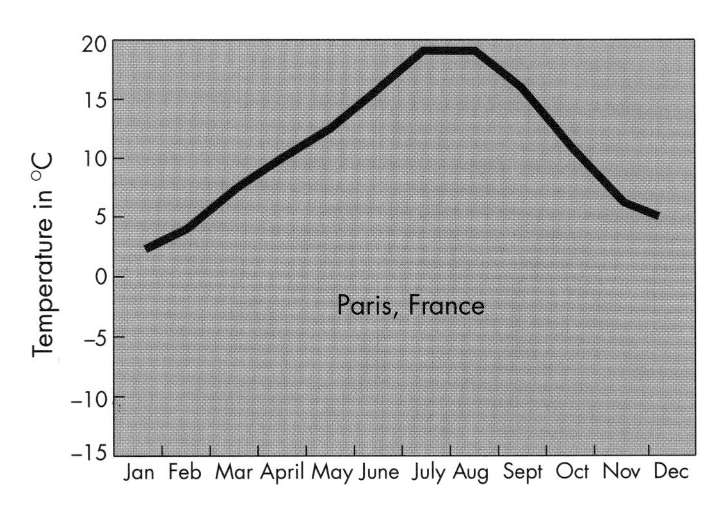

These two graphs show the yearlong temperatures for Paris and Stadacona (present-day Quebec City). Using the graphs, explain why Cartier and his men would have suffered so much during their first winter in America.

SOMETHING TO DO

1. Did the Mi'kmaq and the Haudenosaunee welcome contact with the French? Give some examples of their behaviour to support your answer. What other choices could these Aboriginal peoples have made when they met the French for the first time?
2. In pairs, role-play a meeting between Jacques Cartier and Donnacona. Whoever is playing Cartier has to explain why France has a right to own the land. Donnacona has to explain why the land belongs to his people.
3. Give three reasons why these early French attempts at settlement in Canada failed.

10

acques Cartier had claimed the St. Lawrence River for France, but his attempt to make a settlement there met with failure. Many years passed before any other Europeans tried to repeat Cartier's experiment. Fishers came to catch cod off the coast, and traders visited to obtain furs. But no one came to live the year round, to farm and build communities.

In the early 1600s the King of France decided that it was time to try again. The King knew that it cost a lot of money to build a settlement so far from home. In order to pay for it, he offered a **monopoly** of trade to any merchant who was willing to bring settlers to the St. Lawrence River. The merchant could use profits from the trade to pay the expense of creating a settlement in what the French were soon calling New France.

A French noble named Pierre de Monts received the first monopoly. In 1604 he sailed for New France, taking with him a map-maker and surveyor named Samuel de Champlain. Champlain explored the coast of what is now Nova Scotia and New Brunswick, and the French built a fort at a place they called Port Royal.

Port Royal turned out to be badly placed for the fur trade, so in 1608 Champlain and the French settlers moved to the St. Lawrence River. They settled at the spot where Jacques Cartier had visited the village of Stadacona many years earlier. But the village had disappeared; Donnacona's people were gone. Historians still do not know for sure what happened to them.

Champlain renamed the spot Quebec, from an Aboriginal word meaning "the place where the river narrows." He built a wooden **habitation**, a building that was a fort, a warehouse, and a home. That first winter, 20 of the 28 settlers died from illness and cold. But Champlain and the other survivors hung on, trading for furs and growing the first crops.

Champlain lived at Quebec for 27 years. He explored up the river into the interior of the continent, arriving at the Great Lakes and making friends with the Wendat

DID YOU KNOW?

The French called the area around Port Royal Acadia, and the people who came to live there and along the Bay of Fundy were called Acadians. The name Acadia comes from the Greek word *Arcadia*, meaning "an earthly paradise". Later this area became Nova Scotia.

The French habitation at Port Royal was a central courtyard surrounded by wooden buildings. The original structure disappeared over the years. It was rebuilt by the government as an historic site in 1940. People can visit Port Royal to find out how Canada's first colonists used to live.

The Birth of New France

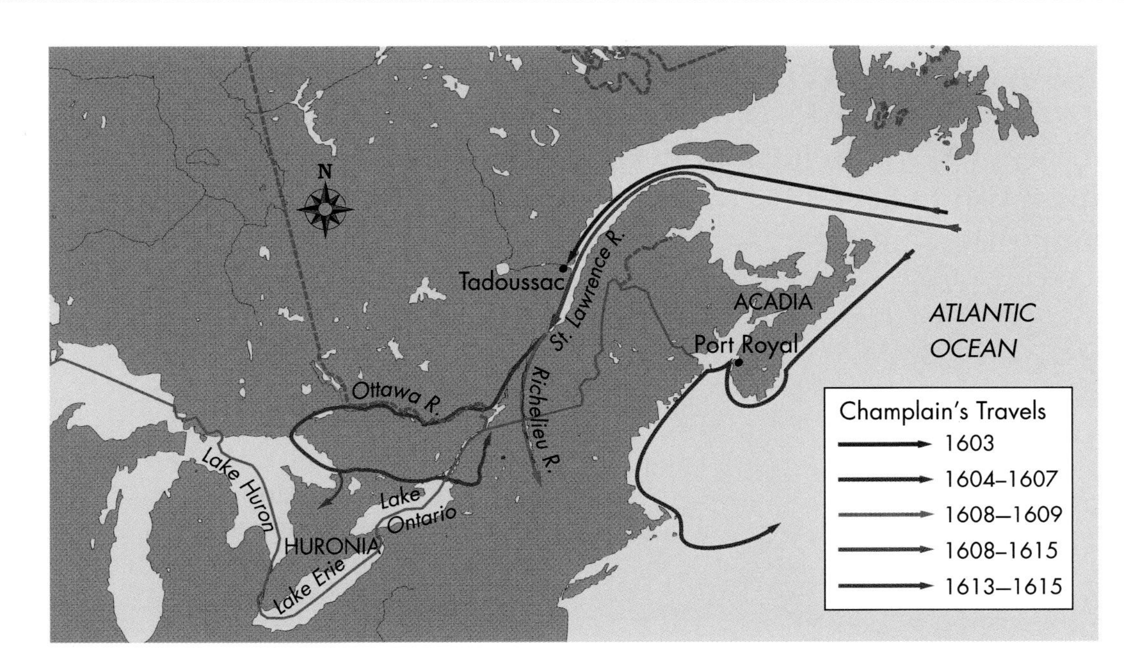

This map shows the parts of New France that Champlain explored.

people who lived there. He convinced the Wendat to bring their furs to Quebec and fought with them against their enemies, the Haudenosaunee.

But Champlain was more than a trader. He was a colonizer. He brought families from France to build farms and villages and establish a permanent **colony**. When he died in 1635, Quebec was still small and struggling, but it was a start. For this reason, Samuel de Champlain is known as the founder of New France.

DID YOU KNOW?

The St. Lawrence was called the river of Canada. It became the "main street" of New France. It was easily reached from the ocean by ships from Europe, and at the same time it stretched for many kilometres inland. It was the main route used by the Aboriginal peoples to bring their furs to trade.

This drawing is the only picture of Champlain that exists. It was made by Champlain himself. It shows him in the centre, firing his musket at a group of Haudenosaunee.

SOMETHING TO DO

1. Do you think Samuel de Champlain deserves to be called the founder of New France? Why or why not?
2. Think back to Jacques Cartier's adventures in Canada. What goals did Cartier and Champlain have in common? Suggest some reasons why Champlain's attempt to form a settlement was more successful than Cartier's.
3. Write a description of the battle scene drawn by Champlain. Decide who won and explain why. Compare the effectiveness of the weapons used by the French and the weapons used by the Aboriginal people.

11

Navigation is the art of finding your way around. When the first explorers arrived in Canada from Europe, they had only the simplest tools to tell them exactly where in the world they were. Some even believed that the world was flat and if they sailed far enough they might fall off the edge.

Explorers set their route across the vast ocean by using a compass that told them in what direction they were going. They also used a quadrant along with the stars or the sun to calculate their latitude and longitude.

Speed was measured using a log line. The log was dropped into the water and the faster it unreeled, the faster the ship was going. Knots were tied in the line at equal spaces. Sailors counted the knots that went out to find out their speed.

This ***astrolabe*** *may have belonged to Samuel de Champlain, who used it to find his location. By sighting along the central pointer, a navigator could calculate the altitude of a star and determine what latitude he was in. Champlain lost his astrolabe in 1613 along the Ottawa River. It was not found until a farmer dug it up in his field in 1867.*

Sailors measured the depth of the water by lowering a lead line weighted at one end with a piece of metal. When the weight reached bottom, they knew how deep the water was by measuring how much line had gone out.

Ships and Travel

Life aboard the ships was hard. Voyages from Europe to America took many weeks, even months, and were filled with dangers. The ships were small by today's standards. Jacques Cartier's vessel, the Grande Hermine, was only 24 metres long. That's shorter than the distance from home plate to first base on a baseball field. The fierce storms that swept the North Atlantic Ocean might easily send a tiny vessel to the bottom.

Members of the crew were kept busy adjusting the sails, raising and lowering the anchor, pumping water, fixing equipment, scrubbing decks, and keeping a lookout. Boys as young as 10 or 11 joined the crew as ship's boys. They had the lowest rank of any member of the crew. They performed light work and spent a lot of time learning the skills to be a sailor. Women were not allowed to be sailors, although they did travel as ship passengers across the Atlantic at that time.

The sailors slept below deck where the space was dark and airless. Candles were not allowed for fear of starting a fire. A sailor got used to being wet most of the time. Clothes were soaked by spray and there was nowhere to dry them. The crew slept on straw mattresses and each member was allowed to bring along a small chest of personal belongings.

The sailors' meals consisted of beans, hard bread and perhaps some meat or fish. Fresh food went stale very quickly and without fruit and vegetables the sailors became sick with scurvy from lack of vitamins. The longer the voyage, the more sailors got sick.

This timeline, divided into 10-year intervals, shows the dates at which different European explorers sailed across the Atlantic Ocean to America.

Early Explorers to America

Timeline scale: 1490, 1500, 1510, 1520, 1530, 1540, 1550, 1560, 1570, 1580, 1590, 1600, 1610, 1620

- **1492** Christopher Columbus sails across the Atlantic Ocean to America.
- **1500–01** Caspar Corte-Real, a Portuguese explorer, sails to Greenland and Labrador.
- **1523** Giovanni du Verrazzano sails along the coast of North America from Florida to Newfoundland.
- **1534** Jacques Cartier makes his first voyage to the St. Lawrence River.

- **1576** Martin Frobisher makes the first of three voyages to Baffin Island.
- **1585–87** John Davis makes three voyages into Davis Strait, looking for the Northwest Passage.
- **1603** Samuel de Champlain makes his first voyage to the St. Lawrence River.
- **1610–11** Henry Hudson sails into Hudson Bay and spends the winter there. After a mutiny, he is left by his crew to die.
- **1616** William Baffin sails deeper into the Arctic than anyone before him.

SOMETHING TO DO

1. Explain what you think would be the worst thing and the best thing about being a sailor on an early voyage of exploration.
2. Imagine you are a ship's boy on one of Samuel de Champlain's voyages to Canada. Write a letter home to your parents describing what a day at sea was like.
3. Make a timeline (divided into 100-year intervals) to show early contacts between Europeans and Aboriginal peoples. On your timeline, include the arrivals of Leif Ericsson, Christopher Columbus, and Jacques Cartier in America. Beside the name of each explorer, write the Aboriginal group(s) he came into contact with.

DID YOU KNOW?

The crow's nest was a barrel set high up in the rigging at the top of the tallest mast. A lookout scampered up the rigging and stood in the crow's nest keeping a sharp eye out for land or another ship.

It is hard to imagine what the Aboriginal peoples thought when they set eyes for the first time on the strangers from Europe. The two groups were so different. They wore different clothes, believed in different gods, and had different ideas about almost everything. These differences meant that the Aboriginal peoples and the newcomers had a lot to learn about each other. This process of meeting and learning is what is known as the period of **contact**.

This is a drawing of an early meeting between traders and Aboriginal people. Europeans and Aboriginal people were brought together by trade, but they had little understanding of each other's cultures.

When Aboriginal peoples and European newcomers met, each believed themselves to be superior to the other. They judged each other by their own standards. Europeans did not understand that Aboriginal people had their own religions and forms of government. They called the Aboriginal people **heathens** and thought that they lived without laws. Aboriginal people were proud of their ability to hunt and trap and travel effortlessly through the forest. They laughed at the feeble attempts of the Europeans to survive in the wilderness.

As the two groups got to know each other better, they each found things to admire in the other's culture. The Europeans borrowed heavily from Aboriginal culture. They began using **technology** such as canoes to travel on the water, and snowshoes and toboggans to make their way through the forest in winter. They learned to hunt, and even to fight, in the Aboriginal way.

Europeans could not speak the local languages and did not know the best travel routes to the interior. They relied on the Aboriginal people to be their guides and interpreters. And, of course, they relied on the local hunters to bring in the animal furs on which the settlements depended. It is highly likely that the early colonists would not have survived without the help of the Aboriginal people.

For their part, the Aboriginal people borrowed a great deal from the Europeans as well. They quickly saw the advantages of using iron kettles, knives, and axes. They recognized the power of guns and began using European cloth and blankets. Some of them also adopted European religious ideas, becoming **converts** to the Christian faith.

Contact, then, was a process of education and exchange. Unfortunately for Aboriginal peoples it was also often a disaster.

Contact and Cooperation

Unknown to themselves, Europeans brought fatal diseases to North America. Diseases that were common in Europe turned out to be unknown in America. Aboriginal people had never suffered from smallpox, measles, influenza or whooping cough. They had no defenses against them. Hundreds of thousands of people died. Whole villages, even entire tribes, simply disappeared. This pattern was repeated right across the continent, wherever Aboriginal peoples and Europeans met.

As more and more Europeans came to settle in what is now Canada, contact also brought misunderstanding. Newcomers did not always understand how the Aboriginal people used the land, nor did they always respect their customs and beliefs. Europeans believed there was one right way of doing things, the European way. Aboriginal people were forced to give up their lands and they were shunted to the margins of society.

Contact with Europeans weakened the Aboriginal people. Overwhelmed by disease and by new ideas, they lost control over their own lives. However, they did not lose their cultures. With difficulty, Aboriginal groups across Canada adjusted to the newcomers. Even as they adapted to a changing world, they continued to respect their traditional ways. They struggled to preserve their languages and customs and worked to keep their communities together. Eventually their populations began to grow again and they began to seek a new place for themselves as equal partners in the new world.

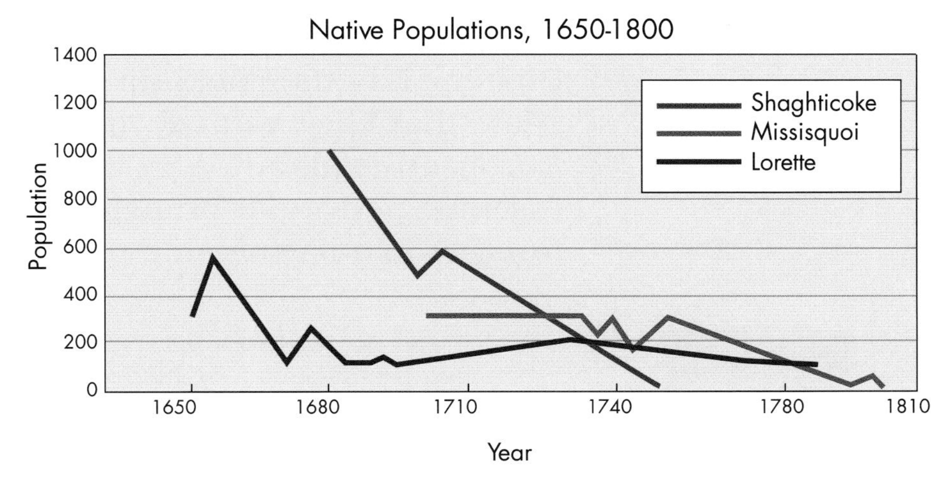

The populations of these three Aboriginal communities dropped sharply from the 1600s to the 1800s. What could have been some of the causes for this?

SOMETHING TO DO

1. In your own words, write one or two sentences explaining what contact was.
2. Compare the advantages and disadvantages of contact from the Aboriginal point of view. Make a chart. In one column include the benefits Aboriginal people received from contact with Europeans. In the other column, write down the drawbacks.
3. Do you have much contact with Aboriginal people? Invite someone from an Aboriginal group in your community to visit your class to talk about his or her people. Before the visitor arrives, write down four things that you wonder about Aboriginal people. Ask the visitor questions. After the visit, write down answers to the things you wondered about.
4. Write a report on one of the European diseases brought to North America and its impact on Aboriginal peoples. To do this:
   a) Write down the five most important questions that you would need to answer in order to write about this topic.
   b) Do some research to find sources of information you could use to answer your questions. These sources could be websites, books, people, museums, etc. Write your report based on this research.

13

hen Jacques Cartier met Mi'kmaq people on the shores of Chaleur Bay they held up animal furs on the ends of sticks to show that they wanted to trade. From the very beginning of European exploration in North America, the fur trade was an essential activity. It brought Aboriginal peoples and newcomers together in a partnership that lasted many years.

The Wellington (1812)

The Regent (1825)

The Paris Beau (1815)

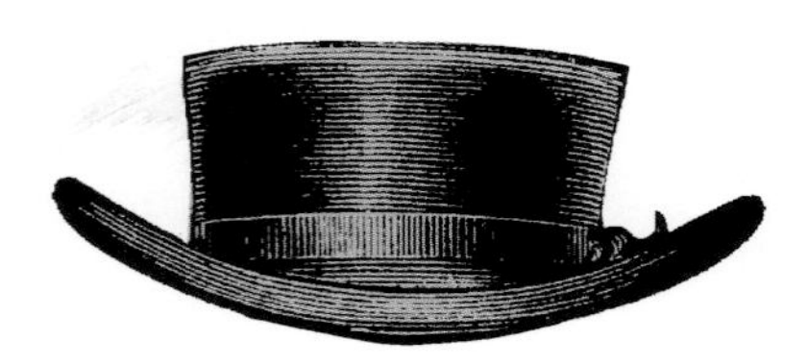

The D'Orsay (1820)

These were the styles of beaver hats worn by fashionable people in Europe. The demand for fur hats kept the fur trade a thriving business.

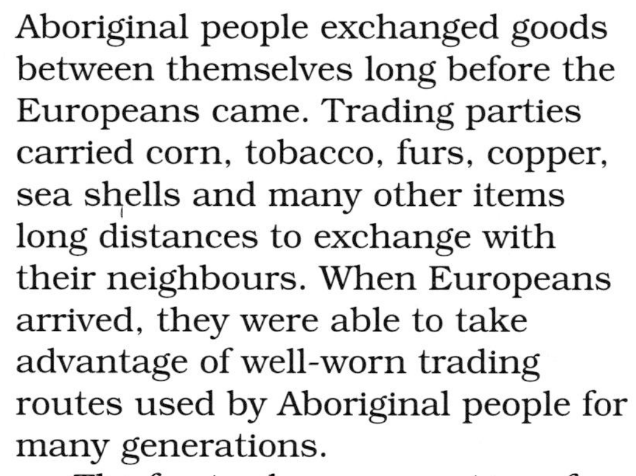

Aboriginal people exchanged goods between themselves long before the Europeans came. Trading parties carried corn, tobacco, furs, copper, sea shells and many other items long distances to exchange with their neighbours. When Europeans arrived, they were able to take advantage of well-worn trading routes used by Aboriginal people for many generations.

The fur trade was a system of **barter**. Aboriginal people did not sell their furs for money. What use was money to them? They had nowhere to spend it. Instead they exchanged the furs for goods offered by the European traders. These goods included kettles, knives, axes, guns, and blankets. Aboriginal people desired these items because they were stronger and lasted longer than the goods they made for themselves out of stone and wood.

Beaver fur has two layers. The outer layer consists of guard hairs, which are long and coarse. The inner layer is fine and smooth, like wool. It was this inner layer, called felt, that was used to make hats.

A system of barter involved a lot of bargaining. A hunter would offer furs for a certain price, perhaps a gun. A trader would suggest that was too much and offer a blanket instead. After bargaining back and forth in this way, hunter and trader usually agreed on an acceptable "price."

The trade for furs took place amid a great deal of ceremony. For the Aboriginal people, trading was part of socializing. Gifts were exchanged, speeches were made and the pipe of friendship was passed from hand to hand. This was the way Aboriginal people had always traded. Europeans were expected to follow the traditional ways.

The fur trade involved three main groups. First of all there were the Aboriginal hunters who trapped in the interior during the winter. They skinned the animals and prepared the furs. When the ice melted in the spring, they loaded their bark canoes and carried the furs down the rivers to the trading posts.

In time, the French traders took over the job of transporting the furs. They learned the skills of paddling the canoes and surviving long trips in the wilderness. These French adventurers were known as ***coureurs de bois*** ("runners of the woods"). They were a unique group created by the fur trade. They lived for long periods among the Aboriginal people. Some even turned their backs on life in the colony and went permanently to live in the villages of the interior.

The third group were the merchants who organized the trade.

The Fur Trade

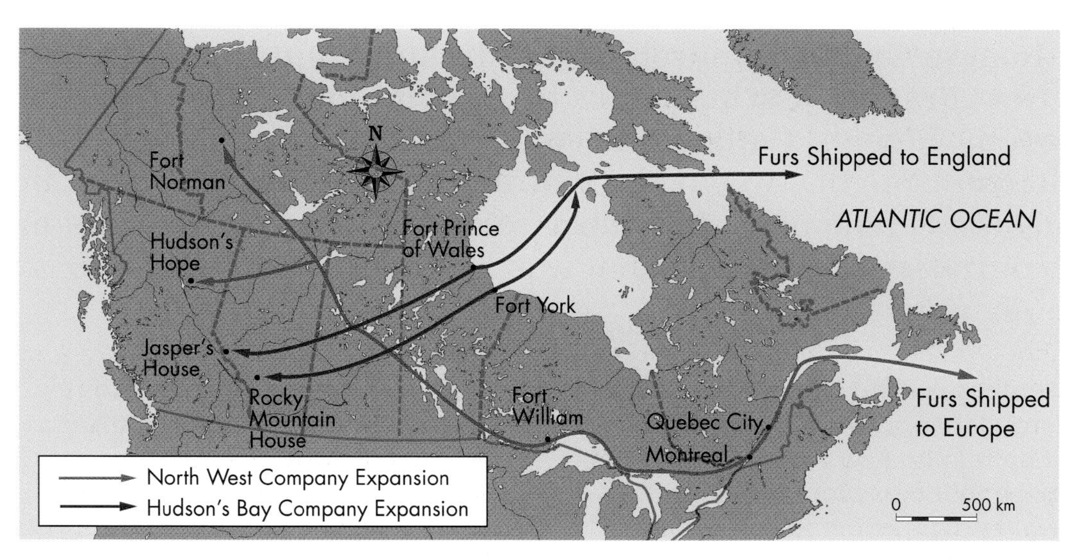

This map shows the flow of furs out of the interior. As you can see from the map, as the search for furs moved north and west, Hudson Bay became closer to the best trading grounds and the St. Lawrence River moved farther away.

They purchased trade goods in Europe, shipped them to New France, and hired the *coureurs* to take them inland. Then they took the furs back to Europe where they sold them to hat makers.

The French were not the only people involved in the fur trade. To the south along the Atlantic coast, English settlers had formed their own colonies, known as New England. They were anxious to lure the Aboriginal people and their furs away from the French. English traders were also active in the north, out of Hudson Bay. In 1670 a group of English merchants, called the Hudson's Bay Company, began building posts and setting up a fur trade system to rival the French.

The fur trade expanded rapidly across the continent. The beaver disappeared from one area after another, and trappers had to move farther north and west to find more furs. It was because of the fur trade that Europeans explored the whole of Canada. Following the river routes shown to them by the Aboriginal people, the fur traders eventually travelled to the Arctic and all the way to the Pacific Ocean.

As Aboriginal peoples who traded furs desired more European trade goods, the need to find more furs became an urgent matter. As a result, whole areas were stripped of beaver and the Aboriginal groups had to move farther afield to find more. This movement displaced other Aboriginal groups, causing disputes between them.

SOMETHING TO DO

1. It is sometimes said that the fur trade created Canada. In your own words, explain what this idea means.
2. Identify aspects of the Canadian landscape and climate that affected the fur trade. Explain the importance of each factor.
3. Make a list of European trade goods mentioned here and others you know about. Opposite each item, list an item used by Aboriginal people for the same purpose. In each case, explain how the new item might have changed the lives of Aboriginal people.
4. Compare the reasons why Aboriginal peoples hunted beaver before the Europeans came and after. What effect did the European demand for furs have on the natural environment, and on the lifestyles of the Aboriginal peoples?

he Roman Catholic Church played an important role in the life of New France, just as it did back home in France. For the French, Roman Catholicism was the one true faith. Most colonists sought the guidance of their priest and took part in religious ceremonies. And most colonists believed that one of the purposes of the settlement was to spread their religion to the Aboriginal people.

Members of the Catholic Church established most of the schools and hospitals in New France. Many of these pioneers were religious women who came to the colonies from France. In 1639, for example, a group of Ursuline **nuns** arrived in Quebec City where they opened a school for girls. One of these nuns was Marie de l'Incarnation. She spent the next 30 years working to educate the young women of New France.

Jeanne Mance was another pioneer. In 1642 she helped to found the village that would become Montreal and opened a hospital there. A few years later Marguerite Bourgeoys came to Montreal to teach school and work among the poor and the sick. She has been called Canada's first social worker.

This portrait of Marguerite Bourgeoys was painted shortly after her death in 1700. The religious group that she established survives to this day.

All these women, and many others, were driven by a desire to see their religious faith brought to New France.

The Church also sent religious workers to spread the Catholic faith among the Aboriginal people. These workers were known as **missionaries** and the small settlements they founded in the wilderness were called missions. Of course, the Aboriginal people had their own religious beliefs. But the missionaries refused to accept that Aboriginal religions had any worth.

The most prominent missionaries in New France were the Jesuits. They arrived in the colony in 1625 and began carrying their religious message to the distant Aboriginal groups of the interior. The Aboriginal people called them "black robes" because of the long, black gowns they wore. They travelled by canoe with Aboriginal guides, paddling long hours under the broiling sun, then sleeping for a few hours under an upturned canoe before setting off again before dawn. This work was not easy and the missionaries had to be as hardy as any *coureur de bois.*

The Jesuits were also explorers. In many cases, they were the first Europeans to travel to the areas they visited. Just as traders spread across the continent in search of new sources of furs, so the missionaries travelled far and wide in search of Aboriginal people to convert to their religion.

The Role of the Church

Ste. Marie Among the Hurons was an important French mission established by the Jesuits. It was the first European settlement in Ontario. The original mission was destroyed, but a replica was built near the present-day community of Midland. Visitors to the site can discover what life was like for the early missionaries.

The main Jesuit mission was in Huronia, the land of the Wendat people, in what is now central Ontario. The Wendat welcomed the "black robes" into their villages for fear that if they did not, the French would stop trading for their furs.

The missionaries believed that they were bringing spiritual truth to the Wendat. Unhappily, their presence had tragic results. Smallpox made its way into Huronia via the missionaries. The disease killed more than half the people and left the Wendat too feeble to resist the attacks of their enemies. Their religious teachings weakened the Wendats' confidence in their own traditions and caused division in the villages.

In the 1640s Huronia came under intense attack from the Haudenosaunee to the south. The Haudenosaunee were running short of furs in their own territory. They wanted to take over the role of the Wendat as chief suppliers of furs to the French. The Haudenosaunee invaded Huronia, burning villages and killing and taking people captive. Several missionaries also died. The few survivors fled back to Quebec.

Huronia was destroyed and for many years the French and the Haudenosaunee were desperate enemies. It was only at the greatest risk that the French ventured inland from their settlements on the St. Lawrence River. Exploration of the interior would have to wait for more peaceful times.

In 1635 the missionary Father Le Jeune wrote this description of a canoe trip to the interior. "You must expect, at least for three or four weeks on the way, to be with people you have never seen before and to be cramped in a bark canoe in an uncomfortable position—in danger 50 times a day of being upset or being dashed upon the rocks. During the day the sun burns you. During the night you run the risk of being eaten by mosquitoes. In the evening the only food is a little corn crushed between two stones and cooked in fine clear water. The only bed is the earth, sometimes only the rough, uneven rocks, and usually no roof but the stars. If you are accidentally hurt, if you fall sick, do not expect any help. Where would it come from?"

SOMETHING TO DO

1. Choose an Aboriginal group and do some research to find out about their spiritual beliefs before the people had any contact with Europeans.
2. How did the French missionaries influence relations between the Wendat and the Haudenosaunee?
3. Jesuit missionaries kept detailed records of their everyday lives. Write a diary entry that a missionary in Huronia might have made. Describe the journey to Huronia and what life is like at the mission.

15

As the fur trade grew, it expanded deeper and deeper into the interior. French missionaries and explorers crossed the Great Lakes and reached the mighty Mississippi River. In the north, rival English traders built posts on Hudson Bay. The fur trade divided the continent between the French and the English, and caused much of the warfare that lasted until 1763.

In 1672 Louis Frontenac became governor of the colony of New France. Frontenac wanted the colony to expand westward to capture the fur trade. He sent out explorers and had a fort built, named after himself, at the site of present-day Kingston, Ontario.

One of Governor Frontenac's favourite explorers was a trader named René-Robert Cavelier de La Salle. During a series of explorations, La Salle travelled into the wilderness beyond the Great Lakes, reaching the banks of the Mississippi River, which flows south all the way to the Gulf of Mexico. In 1682, La Salle reached the mouth of the great river. He claimed the vast territory around for King Louis of France, calling it Louisiana. Louisiana remained French territory for many years.

This map shows the size of New France at its greatest extent.

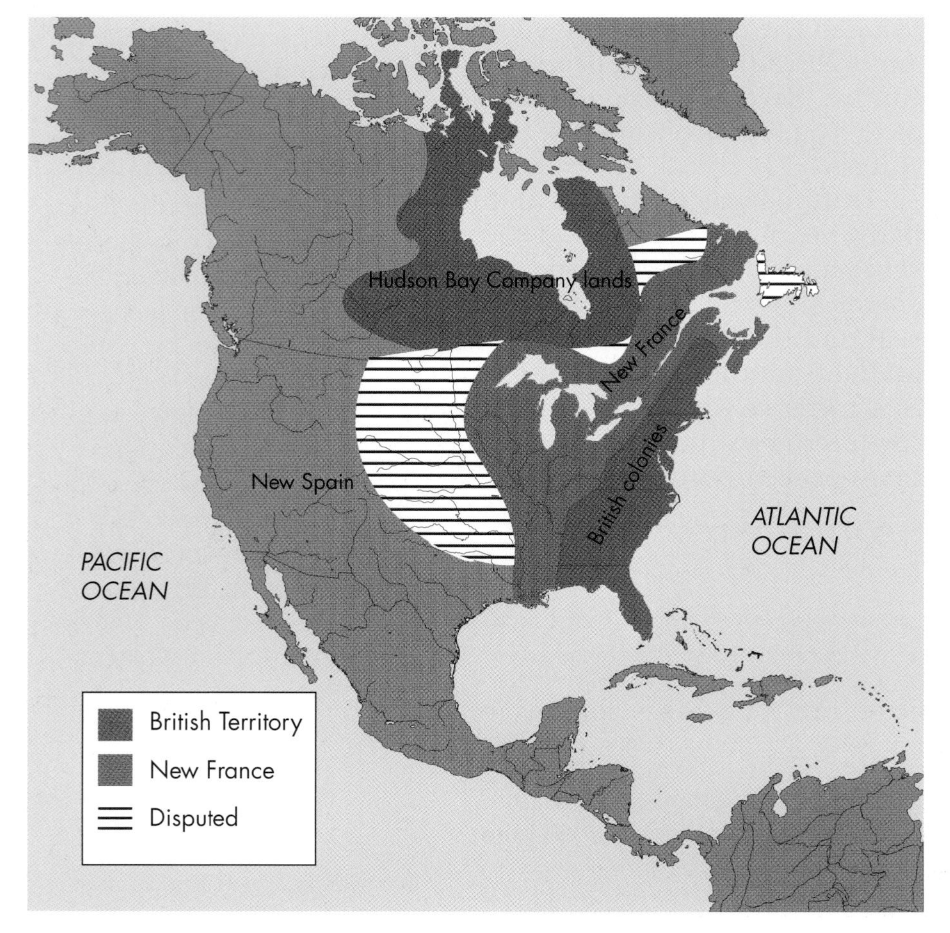

Meanwhile, the French were also expanding into the north. Two of the most adventurous *coureurs de bois* were Pierre Radisson and his brother-in-law, the Sieur des Groseilliers. Together they explored the Great Lakes area in the 1650s, returning to the colony with many furs. The Aboriginal people told the two traders about a large sea far to the north where the country was rich in furs. Radisson and Groseilliers devised a plan to visit this place. When the French authorities were not interested, Radisson took the idea to the English. In 1668 an English ship, the *Nonsuch*, crossed the Atlantic and entered Hudson Bay. A year later the ship returned to England loaded with furs. This voyage led to the creation in 1670 of the Hudson's Bay Company.

The King of England granted the Hudson's Bay Company the right to trade in the huge territory around the bay. This area was called Rupert's Land after Prince Rupert, an English noble. Rupert's Land included much of what we know as western and northern Canada. At the time, no Europeans had ever travelled through it. There were no maps. The officials of the Hudson's Bay Company did not even know how big their territory was.

The English traders established a network of posts in Hudson Bay. They were not interested in forming a colony, as the French had done beside the St. Lawrence. They only wanted to trade for furs. They built their small, wooden forts at the mouths of the important rivers. This is where the Aboriginal hunters came in their canoes each summer to trade.

The trading posts resembled stores in the wilderness. The blankets, guns and tobacco they offered lured many of the Aboriginal traders away from the French. In their competition with the French, the English in Hudson Bay had many advantages. Their posts were closer to the supplies of furs in the forests of the north country. Their ships could bring heavy goods that were difficult for the French to carry in their canoes. The Hudson's Bay Company did not have to spend large amounts of money building a colony. For all these reasons, the English were well suited to compete for furs with the French.

This is what an artist thought a coureur de bois *looked like. In the beginning* coureurs de bois *were actually criminals. The French king wanted New France to develop as a farming colony. He was disappointed when so many young colonists escaped to the woods seeking adventure. The king made it illegal to go trading without a license. But so many traders ignored the law that eventually he had to give up. The* coureurs *were no longer fugitives, liable to be tossed into prison if they were caught.*

This is a sketch of Prince of Wales Fort, one of the trading posts built by the Hudson's Bay Company.

SOMETHING TO DO

1. On a map of modern Canada, find the names of four rivers that flow into Hudson Bay. What provinces or territories are they in? Are there any communities at the mouths of the rivers today?
2. Compare the map on page 32 with a map of North America today. How is the territory of New France different from modern-day Quebec?

16

The competition for furs between French and English traders was a "war" of geography. The French knew that they had to cut off the flow of furs to Hudson Bay. To do this, they built their own posts further up the rivers leading into the Bay. Their plan was to intercept the Aboriginal hunters before they reached the English. This competition led the rival traders all the way across the interior of North America to the Rocky Mountains.

Fur traders and explorers had only a sketchy idea of what the interior of North America looked like. They believed there was a great "Western Sea" not far beyond Lake Superior. If they could reach it, the Western Sea would carry them all the way to China. As it turned out, there was a Western Sea. We call it the Pacific Ocean. But it was much farther away than the early explorers believed.

Of the many traders and explorers who travelled into the interior, three are considered most important for what they accomplished.

1. Henry Kelsey was only 20 years old when he ventured away from Hudson Bay into the interior in 1690. He travelled with Cree guides who led him out of the forests onto the grasslands of the western plains. Not a great deal is known about the two years Kelsey spent living with the tribes of the interior. He probably reached as far west as the modern province of Saskatchewan. He was the first European known to have seen the plains country and also the first to see the vast herds of buffalo that once lived there.

2. Pierre LaVérendrye was a French soldier and a farmer who turned to the fur trade later in his life. He heard stories of the Western Sea and a fabulous land rich in wild animals, silver, and diamonds. He decided to be the first French trader to go there.

LaVérendrye came at the western plains from a different direction than Henry Kelsey. During

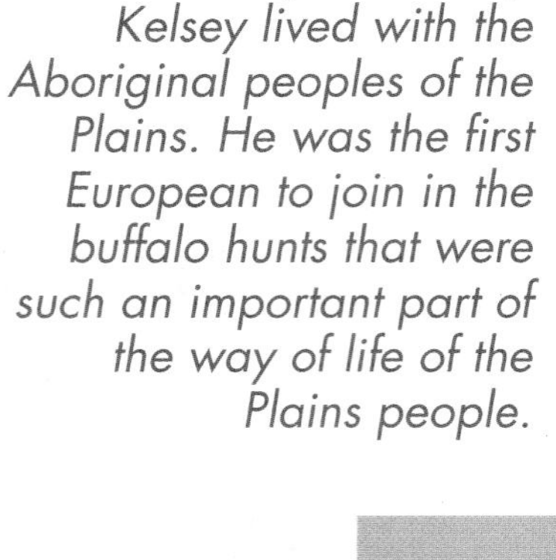

For two years Henry Kelsey lived with the Aboriginal peoples of the Plains. He was the first European to join in the buffalo hunts that were such an important part of the way of life of the Plains people.

the 1730s he made several trips by canoe across the Great Lakes and through the forests of northern Ontario. At last he and two of his sons arrived at Lake Winnipeg where they built a fort. From there they travelled southwest into what is now the United States to visit an Aboriginal people called the Mandans. Later his sons travelled farther west and may have been the first Europeans to see the Rocky Mountains.

LaVérendrye never did find the Western Sea. He did locate the Saskatchewan River, the largest river on the plains. Aboriginal people used it as their main travel route and within a few years it became the most important river in the western fur trade.

3. Anthony Henday visited the plains in 1754. He started from York Factory, where he worked for the Hudson's Bay Company, and he travelled all the way to the modern site of Red Deer, Alberta. The purpose of Henday's expedition was to meet with the Siksika, or Blackfoot, people to try to convince them to bring furs to the Bay.

After a long journey, Henday and his guide, a Cree man named Attickasish, reached a large Siksika camp of about 200 tipis. The chief received them seated on a white buffalo robe surrounded by 20 **Elders**. Pipes of tobacco were passed around and everyone smoked as a sign of friendship. Then they feasted on pieces of boiled buffalo meat served in baskets made of woven grass.

Henday told the Siksika that he had come to invite them to travel to Hudson Bay to trade their furs. But the Siksika told Henday that they had no interest in trading. It was a long journey, they said. They had everything they needed in their own lands.

Henday and his party remained in the west for a winter. When spring came, they returned by canoe to York Factory. His expedition provided much useful information about the Aboriginal groups who inhabited the interior.

York Factory was the main Hudson's Bay Company post. It was located where the Hayes River flows into Hudson Bay. Established in 1684, it is the oldest European settlement in Manitoba. The Hudson's Bay traders called their posts "factories" and the person in charge was called a factor.

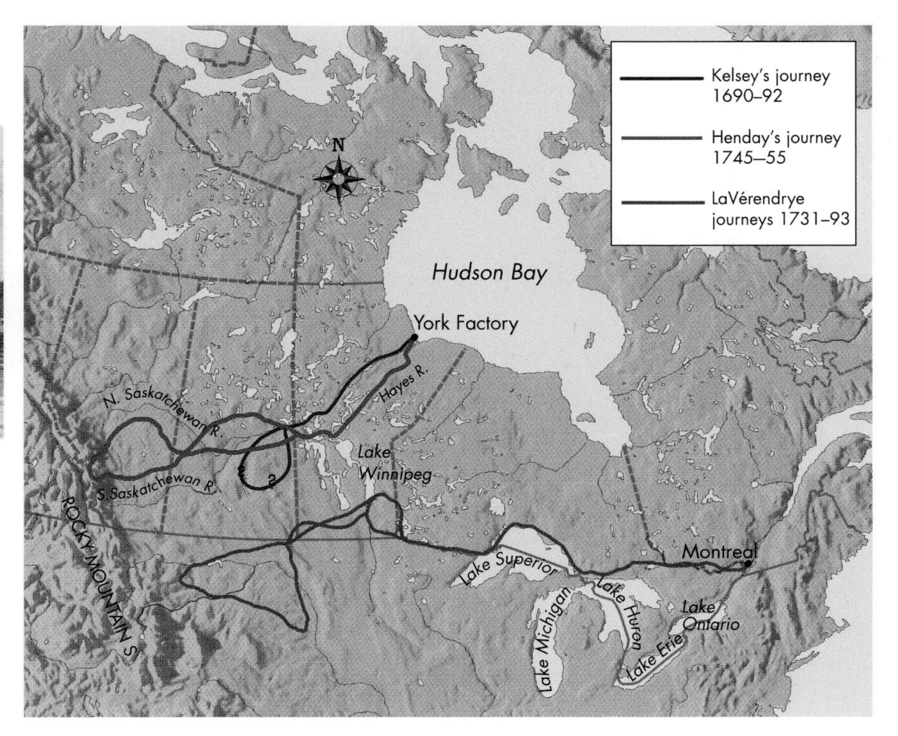

This map shows the routes travelled by the explorers Kelsey, LaVérendrye and Henday.

SOMETHING TO DO

1. Explain how the competition for furs led to the exploration of the interior of North America.
2. Locate York Factory on the west coast of Hudson Bay in your atlas. Explain why it was in a good location for the fur trade. How did trade goods arrive from Europe? How did furs arrive from the interior?
3. Give two reasons why competition between European traders worked to the advantage of Aboriginal people. Can you think of any disadvantages?

17

Travel through the interior would have been impossible without the canoe. Canoes were perfectly suited to the rivers and lakes of North America. Aboriginal people had always used them, and European newcomers right away recognized their value. As Samuel de Champlain wrote: "In their canoes the Indians can go without restraint, and quickly, everywhere, in the small as well as the large rivers. So that by using canoes as the Indians do, it will be possible to see all there is."

This painting shows one of the large canot du maître *plunging through the rapids. It was painted by Frances Hopkins, the wife of a fur trade official. If you look very carefully, you can see Mrs. Hopkins in the painting, seated in the middle of the canoe.*

In the woodlands of eastern and northern Canada, the canoes were made of birch bark. Bark was strong, but at the same time it was light. One person could carry a small canoe made of bark around the many rapids and waterfalls that blocked the interior rivers.

Builders peeled the bark from the birch trees in long sheets. The sheets were sewn together and attached to a cedar frame using tree roots as thread. The seams between the bark sheets were closed with spruce gum that acted just like glue.

One drawback to the bark canoe was that it was easily damaged. It didn't take much of a bump against a sharp rock to burst a hole in the side or bottom. However, one advantage of this type of canoe was that it was easily fixed. Paddlers always carried with them a bundle of fresh bark and some spruce or pine gum to patch the holes.

Canoes came in different shapes and sizes. The bark canoes made by Aboriginal people for getting around in the woods were quite small and could be heft on the shoulders of a single paddler. Fur trade canoes had to be bigger for carrying large quantities of furs and cargo. The largest were called *canot du maître*. They were used for paddling across lakes and along the broadest rivers. They were up to 12 metres long and took six to twelve men to paddle them. They could carry 2,200 kilograms of cargo. In the wooded fur country beyond the Great Lakes, the *canot du maître* was too big to wrestle around the portages so traders used the smaller, *canot du nord*. It was seven metres long, and carried only half the cargo and half the crew.

Bark canoes were not the only kind of canoes used by the Aboriginal peoples. On the Pacific Coast, the people carved their canoes from cedar logs (see page 7). The Ktunaxa (Tu NA ha), or Kutenai, people of the British Columbia interior made blunt-nosed canoes that they used to gather wild rice. And there were many other types. But the bark canoe was the most common form of transportation for the explorers and fur traders.

A break in the canoe route was called a ***portage****. Paddlers had to carry their canoes around a fierce rapid or across a bridge of land between two lakes. They also had to make several trips carrying their cargo on their backs.*

This photograph shows an Ojibwa family with their canoe in northern Ontario. Bark canoes were easily made and easily mended. That is what made them so popular with inland travellers.

SOMETHING TO DO

1. Explain why the canoe was suited to the Canadian landscape.
2. Today's canoes are made from modern materials such as aluminum and fibreglass. What advantages do these canoes have over the bark canoe? Can you think of any disadvantages?

18

he people who paddled the fur-trade canoes were called **voyageurs**. They were the workhorses of the fur trade. Day after day, from before dawn until past sunset, they paddled the freight canoes. During the summer months, they might travel 3000 kilometres, delivering goods to the trading posts and bringing out the furs.

Being a voyageur was dangerous, uncomfortable work. Canoes could easily upset in the turbulent rivers. There were no days off. No matter what the weather—rain squalls, high winds, baking sun—the trip continued. Mosquitoes and black flies were constant pests so the paddlers usually wore their hair long to hide their necks.

At night they slept on the hard ground underneath their canoes. They were up before the sun and put in four hours of paddling before stopping for breakfast. Every hour the canoes paused for a five-minute rest when the paddlers smoked their pipes and washed the sweat from their faces.

The usual diet of the voyageurs was fish and boiled corn or wild rice mixed with pork fat. There was no time for hunting along the way. Once they reached the West they switched to pemmican, the dried buffalo meat that they carried in skin bags. Their costume included leather moccasins, trousers knotted at the waist with a colourful sash, a flannel shirt and a buckskin coat.

This painting shows voyageurs camping for the night at the end of a portage. They will set off canoeing again before dawn.

Life of the Voyageurs

This painting shows the fur trade canoes setting off from near Montreal. They are heading west to the fur country filled with trade goods for the posts there. People from town turned out to wish them a safe trip.

At the portages the canoes were unloaded and carried on the backs of the voyageurs. So was the cargo, carefully packed in 40 kilogram loads. An able-bodied voyageur carried two of these packs on his back as he tramped back and forth across the portage trail. Sometimes these trails were 15 kilometres long, through swamps and up steep hill-sides. To avoid the portage, the voyageurs often hauled their loaded canoes up the rapids with ropes, wading in the ice-cold shallows at the edge of the swirling water.

Friendly competition developed between the paddlers to see who was the fastest. When they came to a stretch of open water, the race began. It was not unheard of for the canoes to race for two days without stopping to cross the vast expanse of Lake Winnipeg.

The western trading posts were too far from Montreal for the voyageurs to make the trip there and back in a summer. Instead, canoes came from both directions and met in the middle at the west end of Lake Superior. The men who lived at the posts brought their furs, while the larger canoes from Montreal brought supplies. For a few days they met at the "grand portage" at Fort William. Once the business was finished, they held a huge celebration to mark the end of another trading season. Then they each headed back the way they had come.

Voyageurs were usually French Canadians from Quebec. They were the first French-speaking people in Western Canada. Some of these people settled permanently in the West. In this way the French language and culture spread right across Canada and continues to be evident today.

SOMETHING TO DO

1. Imagine that you had a chance to interview a voyageur. Write down a list of five questions that you would ask about life on the canoe routes.
2. Write a newspaper want ad: "Voyageurs Wanted". What abilities do you think a voyageur needed? Be sure to list these skills in your advertisement. Illustrate it with a simple drawing or a symbol to represent the voyageur lifestyle. Post the advertisements in your class.

19

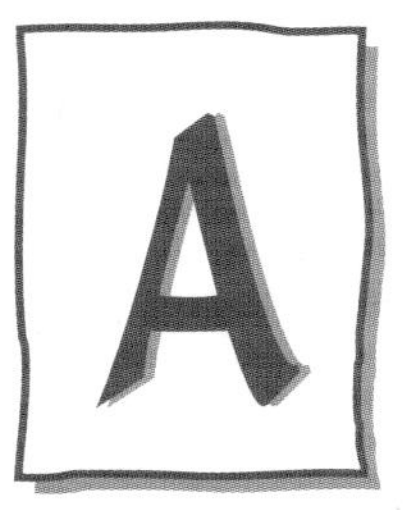

lthough trading posts were built for trading furs, the people who lived in them spent very little time in trade. Small groups of Aboriginal hunters brought in their furs during the winter and in the spring. But mostly life at the trading post was a constant struggle to survive.

What are some of the things you would enjoy about living at a fur trading post? What would some of the hardships be, in your opinion?

The typical trading post looked like a small fort. The buildings were made of logs plastered with mud. The senior traders lived in the "main house," where trading also occurred. The other buildings contained living quarters for the rest of the men, who were sometimes called "servants". There were also storerooms and workshops. Buildings were heated by stone fireplaces, but they were still pretty chilly in the depths of winter when Western Canada went into a deep freeze.

Buildings were arranged in the shape of a rectangle and surrounded by a log stockade. Outside the stockade there was a vegetable garden, a corral for horses and cows, and the "plantation" where the Aboriginal visitors pitched their tents.

The most important activity at

Life at the Trading Post

the trading post was putting food on the table. Parties of hunters went out regularly to shoot bison, deer and game birds, to trap rabbits and to fish. Still, the traders received a lot of their food from Aboriginal hunters. Some of these hunters were paid to hunt full-time for the post.

Other chores included cutting firewood, hoeing and weeding the vegetable garden, keeping the buildings in good repair, and making boats and canoes. Some of the people at the post were skilled tradespeople—blacksmiths, carpenters, gunsmiths and coopers (or barrel makers).

The posts were very isolated. Once winter set in and the rivers and lakes froze over, the only way to get around was on foot. There was no news from home, no visitors to bring word from the outside world. When they weren't working, the men spent their leisure time reading, playing cards and writing letters home that would not be delivered for several months. If they were lucky, there was a fiddler to play some favourite tunes.

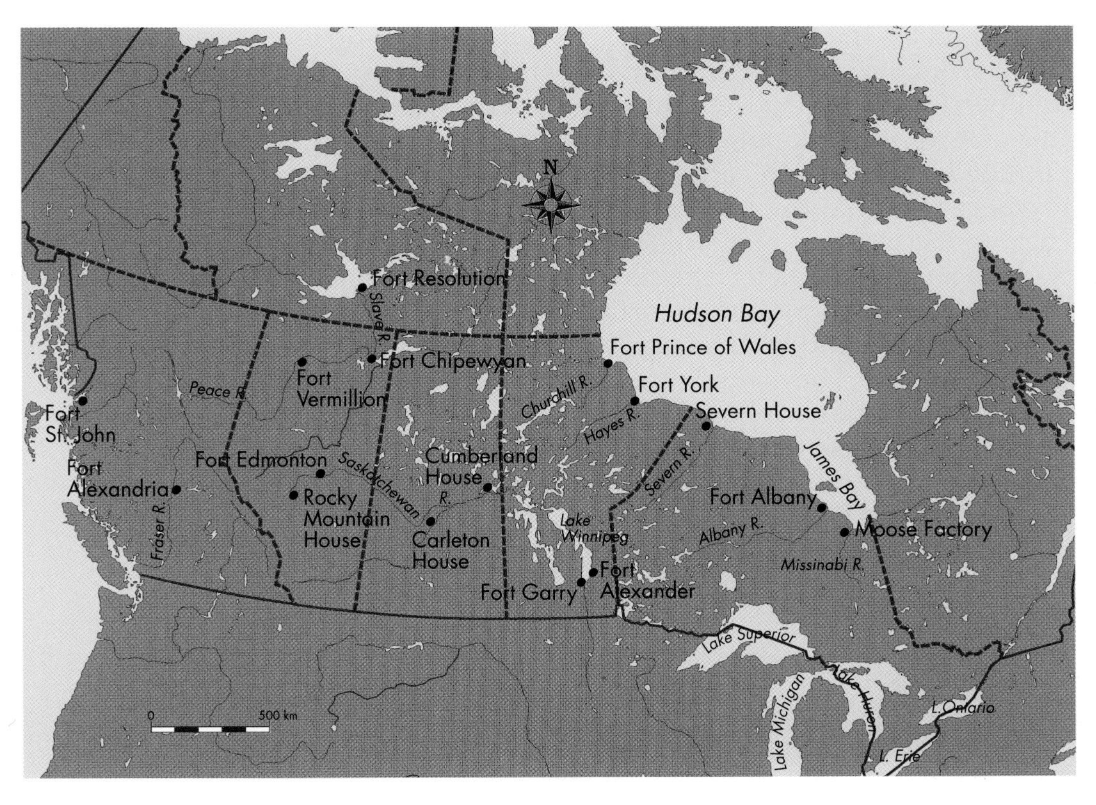

Fur traders built their trading posts all across Western Canada. This map shows the location of some of the most important ones.

SOMETHING TO DO

1. The map shows the location of several trading posts. Why are they all located beside rivers?
2. Keep a journal describing several days in the life of a western fur trader.
3. Make a list of the items Aboriginal people could have received in exchange for their furs. In what ways would these items have improved life for them? Were there any disadvantages to owning any of these items?

A trading post ran according to a strict routine. Here is a description by an early trader.

The servants are rung out and in to duty by a bell. They work from 6 to 6 in summer, and from 9 to 2 in winter, being allowed an hour to breakfast, and the same time to dinner. A regular watch is kept in the night by two men, three hours at a time. The first watch sees all fires and lights out by 9 o'clock. The morning watch lights the fire and calls the men up.

Here is a list of all the wild food eaten at one trading post on Hudson Bay during the winter of 1834-35.

freshwater cod	38
trout	420
whitefish	17 346
other fish	2715
deer meat	3530 kgs
caribou heads	15
caribou tongues	35
ducks	4298
geese	4274
plovers (a shorebird)	3359
ptarmigans	4663
rabbits	816

20

omen played an important role in the fur trade and the exploration of Canada. European women did not come to the fur trade country. The life was considered too difficult for them. But Aboriginal women performed many tasks that made it possible for the newcomers to extend their activities across the continent.

Aboriginal women did all kinds of jobs that assisted the traders. They cleaned the animal skins and used them to sew leather clothing and moccasins. They collected birch bark for making canoes. They wove snowshoes and fishing nets that were used to catch food. They gathered wood for the fires, trapped small animals, and gathered roots and berries to eat. On the prairie they cut up the buffalo meat and pounded it into pemmican, the powdery food that the traders ate on their canoe trips.

When expeditions left the post, Aboriginal women played important roles as guides and interpreters for the Europeans. They could paddle as far as any man, and carry a heavy pack across the portage. They knew the way around the country just as well as their menfolk and could speak several languages. This made them important go-betweens who could make agreements with different Aboriginal groups. When Anthony Henday ventured into the interior in search of the Siksika, one of his guides was a Cree woman.

European traders and explorers often married Aboriginal women. There were no church ministers close by to perform these ceremonies, so the traders called it getting married "according to the custom of the country." The bride's parents gave their permission in exchange for a gift of some kind from the groom—a horse, perhaps, or a pile of blankets. Traders were anxious to marry Aboriginal women as a way of making friends with their wives' family and getting trade from them. A woman might gain influence for her family by marrying a trader. The women taught the newcomers much about the customs of their people.

As a result of these marriages, fur trade posts were filled with children and the noisy activities of family life.

In addition to taking care of the home and family and assisting the fur traders, women took on other important roles as well. For example, an Aboriginal woman named Thanadelthur was an important peacekeeper during the fur trade. You can read about her on the next page.

Picking berries was one of the many jobs that were carried out by women. The food collected by the women would be used to feed the family at home and the fur traders during their journeys.

Women and the Fur Trade

Women were important allies in the fur trade and the exploration of the continent.

THANADELTHUR

The traders in Hudson Bay were anxious to make contact with the Dene people who lived to the northwest. The land of the Dene was rich with beaver, but the Dene did not like to make the trip to the shores of the bay.

In 1714 Thanadelthur, a young Dene woman, appeared at one of the Hudson Bay forts. She had been a captive of the Cree, who were the enemies of the Dene, but she escaped. She offered to try to make peace between the Cree and her people so that the Dene would not be afraid to come to the bay.

Thanadelthur and a trader named William Stuart led a group of Cree people back to Thanadelthur's own territory. She succeeded in convincing the two sides to make peace with each other. William Stuart reported that the success of the mission was all due to Thanadelthur.

The young woman told the traders of rich gold and copper mines in the country of the Dene. But before she could lead the way, she fell ill and died. The chief trader at the post called her one of the bravest people he had ever known.

SOMETHING TO DO

1. Women played an important role in the fur-trade family. What role do you play in your family? Make a list of the duties that you are expected to carry out.
2. Thanadelthur played an important role in Canadian history. Research the life of another important Canadian woman. She might be someone from the past, or someone who is living today. Present your biography in the form of a poster. The poster should have a drawing or photograph of the person, along with some basic information about her life. It should explain why you think this person is important. When everyone puts up their posters around the class, you will have a "Hall of Fame."

DID YOU KNOW?

Isabel Gunn was a young Scottish woman who came to the fur country in 1806. The Hudson's Bay Company would not hire women, so Isabel disguised herself as a young man. She worked in the fur trade for a year and a half without her employers suspecting. They only found out when she gave birth to a baby! After that she and her infant son had to return to Scotland.

Then Europeans began arriving in America, they mixed with the Aboriginal people. European men and Aboriginal women often married. The children of these marriages were a mixture of both backgrounds. They were known as "mixed bloods," or by a French word, **Métis**, meaning a mixture of backgrounds.

This painting of a Métis man and two women dates from the 1800s. It shows the unique clothing styles that were part of the Métis culture. A lot of their clothing was decorated with beadwork, and sometimes they were called "the flower beadwork people".

The Métis developed their own unique way of life. They did a little farming, but mainly they worked in the fur trade and took part in the buffalo hunt on the Western Plains. Meat from the hunt was used to feed the traders at the fur posts. The Métis even spoke their own language. It was called *michif* [me-SHEEF] and was a mixture of Cree, French and Ojibwa [o-JIB-wah].

The Métis buffalo hunt was a very special event. During hunting season the Métis families travelled out on the plains where the buffalo were grazing on the lush grass. They elected their own council to organize the hunt and set the rules by which it was carried out. They also chose a set of captains, who were usually the finest hunters and warriors. The captains were the leaders of the hunt.

When the buffalo were sighted, the hunters mounted their horses and rode into the middle of the herd. As the frightened buffalo stampeded to escape, the hunters chased them, firing their rifles and reloading as they galloped at break-neck speed.

After the hunt the women butchered the carcasses. Back at camp they spread the meat out to dry. Then they pounded it into flakes and made the pemmican, which was so important in the diet of the fur traders.

The Métis in Western Canada saw themselves as a separate people. By the 1870s, with the arrival of European farmers and

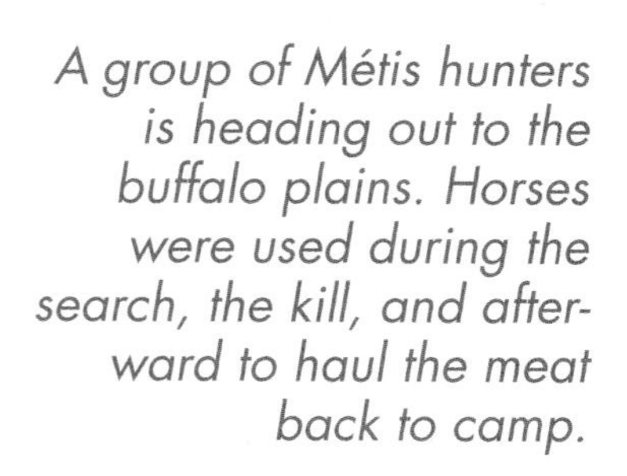

A group of Métis hunters is heading out to the buffalo plains. Horses were used during the search, the kill, and afterward to haul the meat back to camp.

Who Are the Métis?

This photograph shows a group of Métis camped on the plains. The wagons with their large wooden wheels were called Red River carts. They were used by the Métis to carry their possessions and to haul buffalo meat after the hunt. Long caravans of these carts used to cross the plains, raising great clouds of dust.

hunters in the West, the buffalo were disappearing and the Métis began to worry about the arrival of new settlers in their territory. They wanted their own homeland where their culture, language and traditions would be respected.

Led by Louis Riel, the Métis organized to protect their lands against the European settlers who were moving in. They drew up a List of Rights that they sent to the Canadian government in Ottawa. One of the items on the list was that the area they called Red River should become a province of Canada. The government agreed and in 1870 the province of Manitoba was created.

During the years that followed, many Métis families spread west and north onto the plains. There they formed communities and lived by farming as the buffalo disappeared. Again, new settlers threatened to take over their lands. In 1885 the Métis once again asked Louis Riel for help. The dispute ended in violence and the Métis were defeated. Riel was found to be disloyal to Canada, declared a **traitor** and hanged.

In the end, the Métis were pushed aside by the newcomers. They lost most of their land. But they survived as a separate people with a proud history. When Canada made its new Constitution in 1982, the Métis were declared to be one of the three groups of Aboriginal peoples, along with the First Nations and the Inuit of the north.

SOMETHING TO DO

1. Many books have been written about Louis Riel. Do some research and prepare a short biography of Riel. Try to explain why he was considered a great hero by the Métis people but a criminal by the government at that time.
2. The Métis called themselves a "new nation." What does this term mean to you? In what way were the Métis a "nation"?

DID YOU KNOW?

In 1996 the census showed that there were 210 190 Métis people living in Canada.

22

or many years, fur traders on Hudson Bay heard stories about rich gold and copper mines on the shores of a distant river. To reach these mines the traders would have to cross the Barren Lands. These were the vast tracts of northern marshland where it was too cold for trees to grow.

In 1770 the Hudson's Bay Company chose one of its traders to explore the Barren Lands. He was Samuel Hearne, a 24-year-old sailor who worked on the company's trading boats. The purpose of his expedition was threefold:

- to find the rumored mines
- to make contact with distant Aboriginal groups who might have furs to trade
- to continue the search for the Northwest Passage through the Arctic Ocean.

Samuel Hearne did not set off alone. In fact, he was not even the leader of the expedition. That role belonged to a Chipewyan man named Matonabbee [mat-uh-NAH-bee]. Hearne had made two earlier trips into the Barrens. Both trips had ended in failure. Matonabbee told him that no expedition could succeed without good guides and many women to cook the meals, carry supplies and look after the camp. He offered his services as a guide and interpreter.

The party left Hudson Bay in the middle of winter. They travelled by snowshoe, hauling their supplies on toboggans. For a while they travelled with a caribou herd so that they would have plenty to eat. In spring, when the ice melted, the Chipewyan stopped to make bark canoes to carry them across the rivers and lakes.

At one point it was time for a Chipewyan woman who was pregnant to give birth. The party halted for two days. As soon as the baby was born, the trek resumed. The new mother bundled the baby on her back and set off with the rest.

This map shows the route of Samuel Hearne's trek from Hudson Bay to the Coppermine River. It also shows the treeline. This is the line that shows how far north trees will grow.

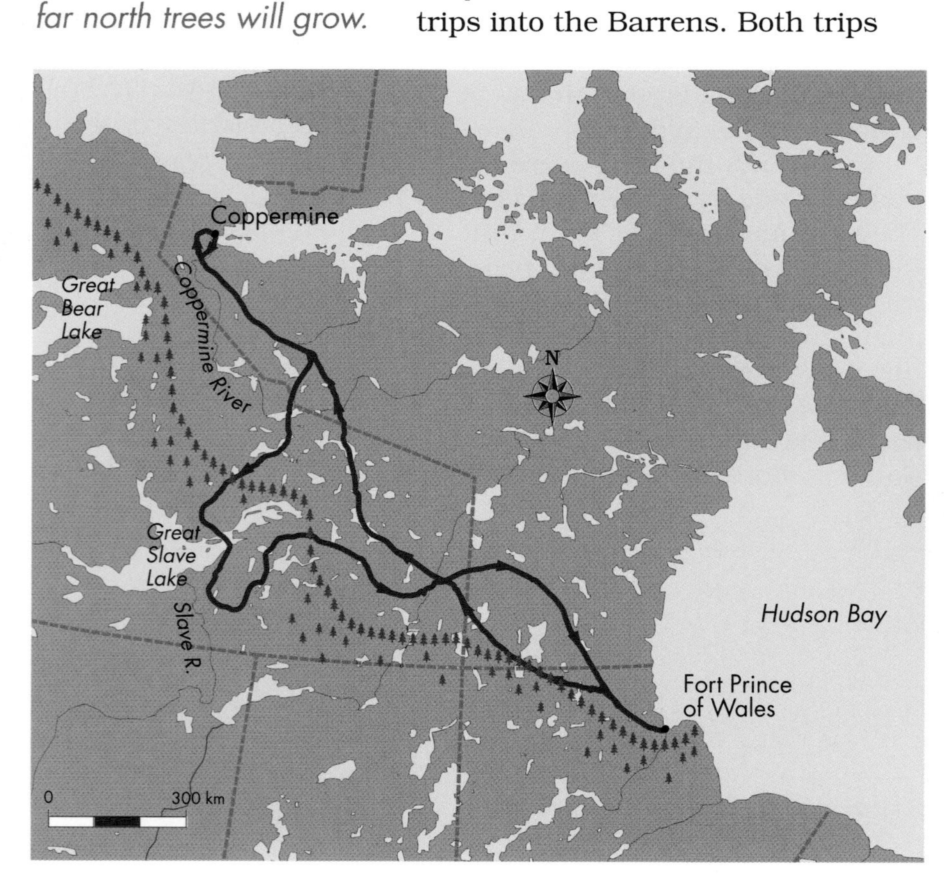

Samuel Hearne

Crossing the Barrens

Along with the child, the mother was expected to carry her usual load!

At the end of May the travellers passed across the edge of the tree-line. Now they were on the Barren Lands. A steady rain fell, soaking their clothing. They slept at night in puddles of water. At last they came to the Coppermine River and found the place where the mines were supposed to be. But all they found was a jumble of rock and gravel. Hearne was very disappointed.

Hearne had completed his mission, but his journey home took almost another year. After thousands of kilometres of walking, his feet became bruised and sore. "I left the print of my feet in blood almost at every step I took," he later wrote.

September came and the party set up camp while they hunted caribou to make skin clothing for the coming winter. They also made snowshoes and sleds for the rest of their voyage.

Setting off again, the party trudged wearily back toward Hudson Bay. It took all winter. Finally, on 30 June 1772, Hearne and his Chipewyan guides reached the trading post at Prince of Wales Fort. They had been gone almost 19 months.

Hearne did not succeed in finding the treasure mines. But during his long trek he did find out some important things.

- He gathered information about the Chipewyan and other Aboriginal groups who lived in the Barren Lands.
- He was the first European to cross overland to the shores of the Arctic Ocean.
- He learned how important it was to have Aboriginal guides when travelling in the interior.

After his years as a fur trader, Samuel Hearne returned to live in England. He wrote a book about his travels. It was called *A Journey from Prince of Wales's Fort, in Hudson Bay, to the Northern Ocean*. In it, he called Matonabbee, his guide, "the most sociable, kind and sensible Indian I had ever met with. He was a man well known and generally respected."

A party of travellers in mid-winter.

SOMETHING TO DO

1. Samuel Hearne pioneered a way of travel that depended on going in the company of Aboriginal people. Instead of taking along food with him, he lived off the land, just as the Aboriginal people did. List the ways in which Hearne "lived off the land."

2. Find out all you can about the caribou. Try to answer these questions: What do caribou eat? Where do they live? Why do they move from place to place depending on the seasons? How did the Aboriginal people use the caribou? Draw pictures to illustrate your findings.

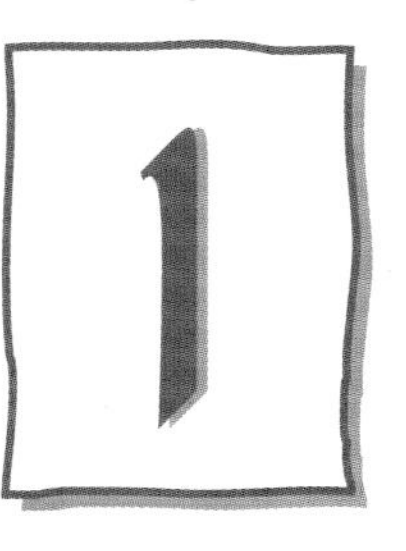

nuit people have lived in northern Canada for thousands of years. During that time, they developed a unique way of life. It was a way of life that allowed these people to make a home for themselves along the coast and on the islands of the Arctic Ocean.

DID YOU KNOW?

The word **Inuit** [IN-yoo-eet] means "the people." The language of these people is called **Inuktitut** [in-UK-ti-tut]. A single Inuit person is called an **Inuk**. In the past these people were known as Eskimos. Today there are about 41 000 Inuit living in Canada.

The Arctic is a land of long, cold winters and short, cool summers. For three months of the year, the sun never rises above the horizon; it is dark 24 hours a day. On the other hand, in the middle of the summer, it is light for 24 hours a day.

The Arctic climate is extreme. In the winter, ice forms on the ocean and the ground freezes. Nevertheless, many forms of life are able to survive. The seas are rich in fish, seals, and whales. There are no trees, but every summer the **tundra** blooms, providing food for the vast herds of caribou that come north.

The Inuit developed a number of tools and weapons that helped them to survive in this extreme place. They built light seal or caribou skin boats, called **kayaks**, that travel swiftly across the water. On land they used sleds and toboggans pulled by dogs. They used animal bone and stone to make harpoons, knives, and scrapers. Their winter houses, called igloos, were made out of blocks of hard-packed snow and kept the people warm in even the coldest weather.

During the winter, many Inuit hunted seals through holes in the ice. In the summer they relied on the caribou. Caribou provided meat for the people, as well as skins for making clothing and bones and antlers for making tools, sled runners and tent frames.

Like the other Aboriginal groups, the Inuit used the resources in their environment to meet all of their needs.

People of the Far North

The Inuit met the European explorers when they began arriving in the Arctic. The explorers came in ships, hoping to find a sea passage around the top of North America. They called this route the Northwest passage, and it was many years before they found it. Meanwhile, the Inuit helped the explorers in their attempts to survive in the extreme climate. They taught the outsiders to eat nutritious seal meat, to dress for the cold in caribou furs, and to use dogs and sleds for travel.

The Inuit took part in the fur trade, just like the Aboriginal peoples farther to the south. Because beaver did not live in the Arctic, traders ignored the area for a long time. But, by the year 1910, white fox furs became very valuable. The Inuit specialized in trapping this animal. Trading posts spread quickly across the North.

Traders were followed by other outsiders who came into the Arctic in search of oil and other minerals. It is only in the past 50 years that non-Inuit have been living in large numbers in the Inuit lands.

*This stone pillar, called an **inukshuk**, was built by the Inuit. It was meant to confuse the caribou, who mistook it for a person and ran in another direction where hunters were waiting. Inukshuks were also put up as markers to guide travellers.*

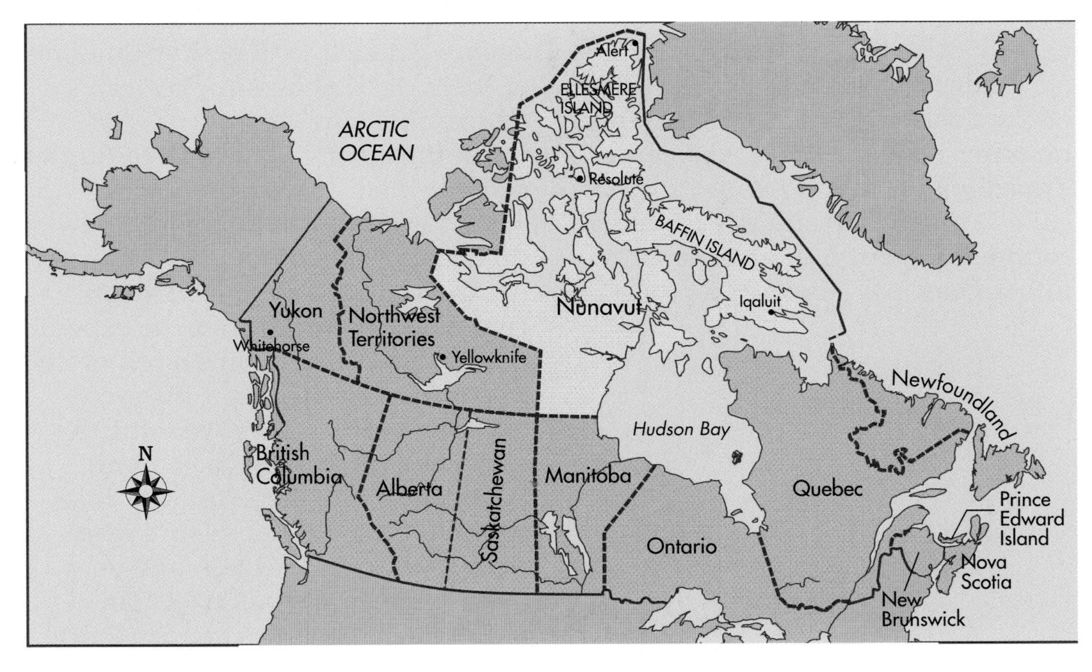

This map shows the territory of Nunavut, created in April 1999.

SOMETHING TO DO

1. List the materials the Inuit used to make each of the following: their winter houses; their clothes; their kayaks; their harpoons.
2. Wood was a very valuable product for the Inuit. Explain why wood was so valuable in the Arctic.
3. In the winter the Inuit hunted seals. But the seals lived in the water under the ice. How did the Inuit hunt them? Do some research to find out about Inuit hunting methods, then draw a picture showing how hunters killed the seals.
4. Do some research to find out why the Inuit people created their own territory, Nunavut.

Nunavut

On 1 April 1999 a new territory was created in Canada. It was called Nunavut. The people living there elect their own **government**, but the government does not have as many powers as a province.

In the Inuit language, Nunavut means "our land." It contains about 20 percent of all the land in Canada. Most of the 25,000 who live in Nunavut are Inuit.

24

rom the time that Christopher Columbus arrived in America, European explorers were seeking a way around the continent. They wanted to be able to sail directly to the rich spice lands of Asia. They called the route they were seeking the Northwest Passage.

Wooden sailing ships used by the explorers offered weak protection from the Arctic ice. When large chunks of ice closed around a ship, they could crush its hull easily and send it to the bottom.

Many explorers sought the Northwest Passage in the frozen waters north of Canada. One of these adventurers was Henry Hudson. In 1610 Hudson was captain of a sailing ship called *Discovery* that came seeking the Northwest Passage off the coast of what is now Labrador. This is where the Vikings had sailed 600 years earlier.

Hudson found a passage of ice-choked water heading west where no other explorer had ever been. Travelling up this passage (it is now called Hudson Strait), the *Discovery* rounded a point of land and sailed into a giant bay, as large as an ocean. This was Hudson Bay and Hudson and his men were the first Europeans to enter it.

Following the shoreline south, the explorers sailed all the way to the bottom of James Bay. There was no time to return to England. Ice formed around the ship as the crew settled in for the winter. Many of the sailors got sick with scurvy and one of them died. Food supplies ran dangerously low.

In the spring, a local Cree hunter came to visit. Hudson traded for some furs, but this was all he saw of the local people. When the ice broke up and the ship could sail again, Hudson announced that the expedition would continue in search of the Northwest Passage. But his crew had other ideas. They were hungry and sick and wanted to go home. Some of them seized Hudson, his son, and seven other sailors who were loyal to the captain and set them adrift in a small boat. The *Discovery* sailed away for England, while Hudson and the others were never seen again.

Freezing cold, starvation, disease—too often these were the fate of the explorers who came in search of the Northwest Passage. The northern waters were a dangerous place for Europeans who did not know how to survive there. For most of the year the ice made any travel impossible. Temperatures plunged well below zero. There was little animal life to hunt for food. Many expeditions ended in disaster.

One of the most famous Arctic explorers was the British sea captain, John Franklin. In 1845 he sailed in command of two ships around the top of Baffin Island, and disappeared. For many years no one knew what had happened. Rescue expeditions were sent to hunt for the lost ships. It was the largest search in Canadian history. In the end it was discovered that the missing ships had become frozen in the ice and sank. Franklin and all his sailors perished.

Despite these tragedies, explorers kept trying to solve the riddle of the Northwest Passage. Finally a Norwegian sailor named Roald Amundsen navigated his small sailboat, the *Gjoa*, through the passage. It took him three years, 1903 to 1906. During the frozen winters he lived on his boat, and for a few months each summer he sailed through the maze of islands and channels. In August 1906 he emerged from the ice, the first person to sail across the Arctic.

For all the many years it took, and lives it cost, the Northwest Passage turned out to be a disappointment. It was too difficult to be used safely by ordinary ships. By the time it was discovered, railways were crossing America and steamships were travelling to Asia. The Passage, once it was found, was unnecessary.

This group of Inuit people was drawn by one of the European explorers. The Inuit helped many expeditions of outsiders to survive in the Arctic, giving them food and teaching them about the land.

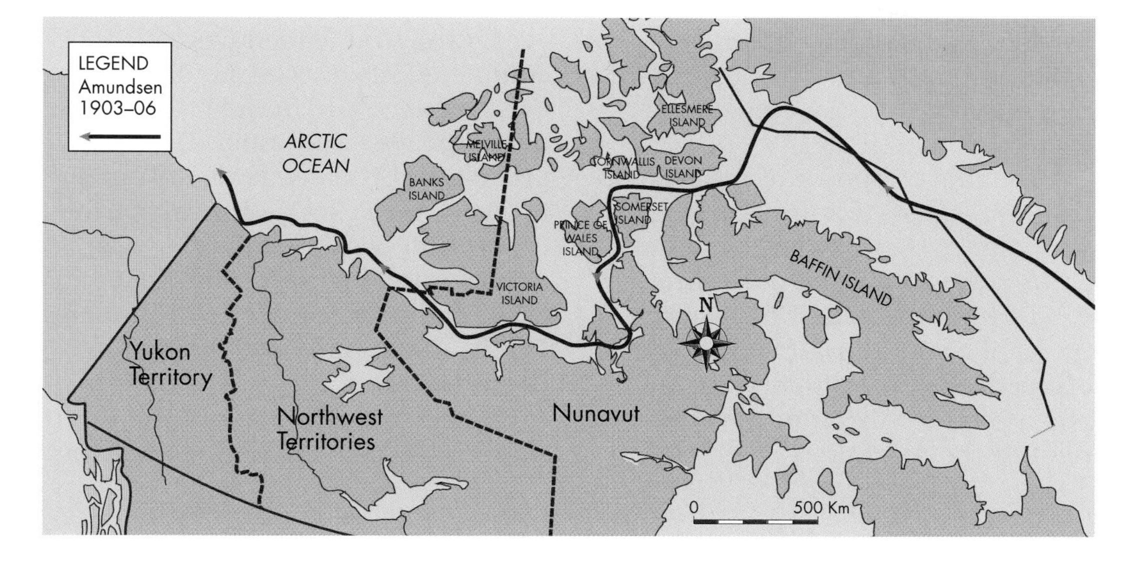

This map shows the route followed by Roald Amundsen on his ship the Gjoa.

SOMETHING TO DO

1. The timeline on page 25 mentions several Arctic explorers. Choose one and prepare a brief biography. Explain how your explorer contributed to the search for the Northwest Passage.
2. Prepare a chart showing the differing points of view of Henry Hudson and his crew. On one side of the chart write down the reasons why you think the crew did not want to continue the voyage. On the other side of the chart, write down why you think the captain wanted to continue on. What would you have wanted to do?

Roald Amundsen wrote about his feelings at the end of his voyage.

"The Northwest Passage had been accomplished—my dream from childhood. This very moment it was fulfilled. I had a peculiar sensation in my throat. I could feel tears coming to my eyes."

[Source: Roald Amundsen, The North West Passage, vol. 2, New York, E.P. Dutton, 1908, p. 125]

25

ost of the European vessels looking for the Northwest Passage began their search in the frozen waters north of Newfoundland. This was the part of the Arctic that was closest to Europe. However, if the passage truly existed, there must be another entrance at the west side of the continent. The search for this entrance lured the first explorers to the part of Canada that is now British Columbia.

British Columbia is a long way from Europe. It is cut off from the rest of North America by several ranges of snow-capped mountains. Because it was so remote, it remained a blank spot on European maps for many years. While traders, and then settlers, were active in the rest of Canada, British Columbia was one of the last regions of the country to be explored.

The first outsiders to arrive were Spanish sailors, who travelled north from their settlements in Mexico in the 1770s. They were followed by British, Russian and American ships. All of them were eager to find new trading partners and explore the rocky coastline.

The most important of the early explorers was Captain George Vancouver. He was sent by Great Britain to explore the coast from California to Alaska. This would prove once and for all whether one of the deep coastal inlets was actually a passage through the continent to the Atlantic.

Captain Vancouver and his crew spent three summers on the coast from 1792 to 1794. They cruised north on their ship, *Discovery*, making maps and using small rowboats to look into every cove and inlet along the way. They gave new names to many of the places they visited, not caring that the Aboriginal people had their own names that they had used for generations. Years later Captain Vancouver's own name was taken by the city of Vancouver that arose on the shores of a deep inlet that he explored.

By the time Vancouver completed his survey, he had drawn the first accurate map of the shoreline of British Columbia. He also proved that there was no entrance to the Northwest Passage along the coast. And perhaps most importantly, he made sure that other countries understood that the Pacific Coast had been claimed by Great Britain.

However, no one asked the First Nations people who had been living

This is a painting of the ship George Vancouver used to explore the coastline of what is now called British Columbia.

there for many generations. As far as the Aboriginal people were concerned, it was their land. This difference of opinion about who has a right to the land remains an important issue today.

When European sailors arrived on the Pacific Coast, they began trading with the Aboriginal groups living there. In the rest of the country, the trade was mainly for beaver skins. On the coast, however, the most valuable fur belonged to the sea otter.

Sea otters live in the ocean along the coast where they feed on sea urchins, shellfish and starfish. They have very thick fur which they need to keep warm and buoyant in the water. During the period 1790 to 1820 it was the most valuable fur in the world, worth about 10 times more than a beaver. It was so valuable that traders called the sea otter "soft gold."

Sea otters were in such demand that they were wiped out on the coast of British Columbia. In the 1960s some animals were brought from Alaska to Vancouver Island to start a new colony. Now hundreds of sea otters once again live along the British Columbia coast. Even so, they are still considered to be an **endangered species**.

This group of Aboriginal leaders is based on drawings made by Spanish explorers in 1792. The man on the right was Chief Tetacu. Next to him, cradling a child, is his wife, who the Spanish called Maria. At the bottom left is Maquinna, chief of the Mowachaht people who lived on the west coast of Vancouver Island. The Mowachaht welcomed the first explorers and traders.

Sea otters float on their backs and carry their young on their stomachs, like a raft. They are one of the few animals in the world to use tools. When they find shellfish, they crack open the shells with a stone.

SOMETHING TO DO

1. The sea otter is an endangered species. Explain what this phrase means. Other endangered species in Canada include the beluga whale, the Vancouver Island marmot, the eastern cougar, and the wood buffalo. Choose one of these animals and find out all you can about it. Where does it live? What does it eat? Why is it endangered? Collect or draw pictures of your animal. You might mount a display on endangered animals in your classroom.
2. Explorers often gave names to places and physical features that they passed on their travels. These names replaced Aboriginal names on European maps. Perhaps your own community, and different lakes and rivers and other physical features in your part of the country, got their names this way. Make a list of some places and features close to where you live and find out how they got their names. Try to find out if the local Aboriginal people know these places by other names.

26

While the sea-otter traders were cruising the coast of British Columbia, other traders were trying to find a route to the Pacific Ocean from the interior. For many years they had been trading furs with the Aboriginal people of the plains and the woodlands. But the Rocky Mountains formed a high barrier that kept the traders out of the interior of British Columbia.

The explorer who finally solved the riddle of the mountains was Alexander Mackenzie. Mackenzie was born in Scotland and came to Canada to work in the fur trade when he was only 15 years old. He belonged to a group of traders called the North West Company. Based in Montreal, this company was a rival of the Hudson's Bay Company. It operated many trading posts right across the continent.

Alexander Mackenzie

Mackenzie was living at Fort Chipewyan when he heard about a great river that was supposed to flow west into the Pacific. This was of great interest to the traders. If they could find a route to the ocean, they could use it to transport their furs to market much more cheaply than carrying them across the continent.

In 1789 Mackenzie set off for the great river with four voyageurs and several Chipewyan guides. Fooled by misleading maps, Mackenzie followed the river as it flowed north instead of west. After many days his expedition arrived at the mouth of the river to find it blocked with ice. They realized they had arrived not at the Pacific, but at the Arctic Ocean.

Disappointed, Mackenzie returned to Fort Chipewyan. Later, the river would bear his name, the Mackenzie, the longest river in Canada. He was the first European to paddle its entire length.

Three years later, in 1792, Mackenzie set out in search of the Pacific for a second time. This expedition was much more difficult than the first. He and his party travelled up the Peace River toward the Rocky Mountains. They paused for the winter at a small trading post, then set off again in the spring. They crossed the mountains carrying their heavy packs, climbing up narrow trails over high cliffs and camping in the snow.

Guided by Aboriginal people, Mackenzie struggled across the mountains. At the Fraser River, which at that time had no European name, he met some local people who offered to show him the way to the ocean. He left his canoes and proceeded on foot along one of the **grease trails** used by Aboriginal groups to trade.

After many days' hiking, the expedition reached the Bella Coola River. They followed it down into a deep inlet. Here Mackenzie tasted salt water and knew he had reached the

DID YOU KNOW?

Grease trails were footpaths leading from the coast of British Columbia to the interior. They were used by Aboriginal people to trade between the different groups. One of the most important items of trade was the oil from a fish called the eulachon. This oil was considered a delicacy by the people. This is why the trails became known as the Grease Trails.

First Across the Rockies

It was only at great risk that the explorers made their way through the mountains. Luckily, their Aboriginal guides knew the country well and showed them the proper routes to follow. Sometimes the canyons were so steep there was no trail at all. The travellers had to creep along like spiders on a wall.

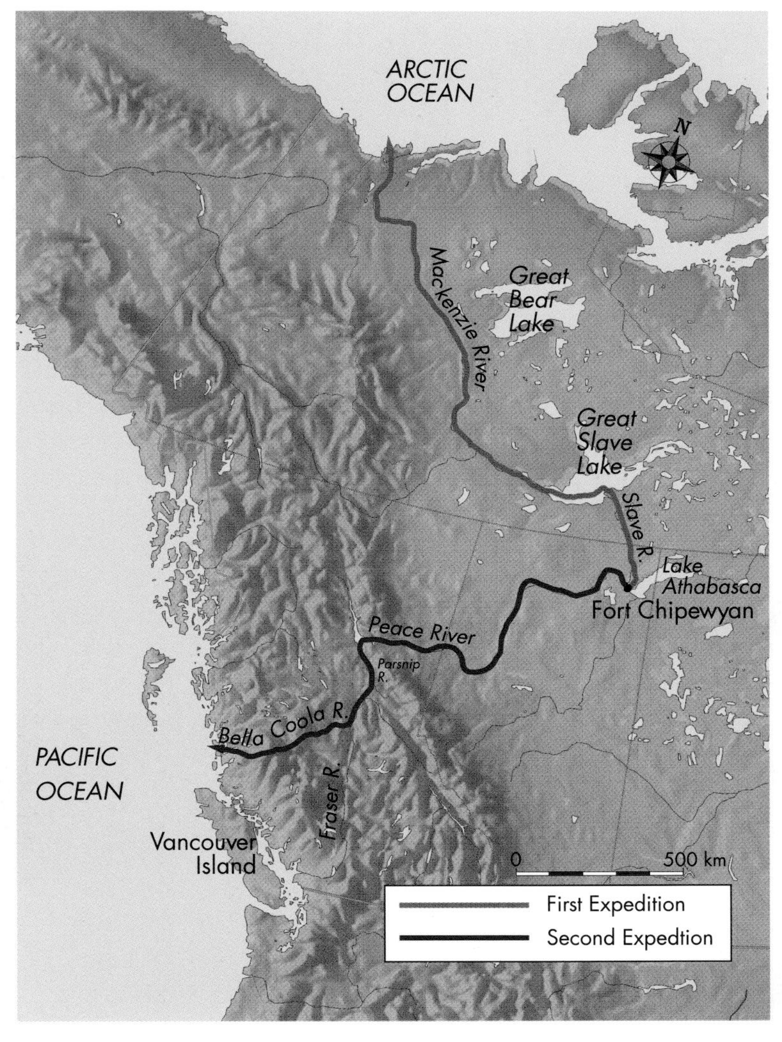

This map shows Alexander Mackenzie's two great expeditions in search of the Pacific Ocean.

ocean. He and his party paddled a few kilometres down the inlet. When they reached the ocean, they ran out of time and had to turn around and begin their journey home. Mackenzie did not know it, but only a few weeks before his arrival some of Captain George Vancouver's sailors had been at the exact same spot!

Other traders followed Alexander Mackenzie into the western mountains and began trading there. They discovered other rivers that ran to the ocean and soon British Columbia was added to the map of North America.

When Alexander Mackenzie reached the Pacific, he wrote a message on a rock, using a mixture of animal grease and dye. The message read: "Alexander Mackenzie, from Canada, by land, the twenty-second of July, one thousand seven hundred and ninety-three." Today the spot is a historic site. Visitors can still read the message on the rock.

SOMETHING TO DO

1. Imagine for a moment that you were travelling with Alexander Mackenzie when he came out of the mountains to the Pacific Ocean. Compose your own message that you would leave behind on the rock.
2. After Mackenzie, other explorers looked for a river leading from the mountains to the Pacific. Two of these explorers were Simon Fraser and David Thompson. Choose one of these explorers and do research to find out more about him and his travels. Write a short paragraph about each explorer. Explain how each added to what was known about British Columbia.

he explorers you have read about in this book were people who paved the way for the European settlement of Canada. But not all exploration took place in the past. There are still new frontiers to be discovered, and modern explorers to take up the challenges.

There are few places left on land that have not already been explored. The vast ocean floor, however, has had few visitors so far. People who explore underwater are called **aquanauts**. One of the things they like to look for are sunken ships. The *Titanic* is an example of a ship that many people were interested in finding.

On 14 April 1912, in the middle of the North Atlantic ocean, a huge ocean liner called the *Titanic* plowed into an iceberg in the middle of the night. The collision punched a hole in the steel hull of the ship. The 2200 passengers and crew rushed to the lifeboats as the luxury liner slowly sank into the ocean.

The builders of the *Titanic* said it was unsinkable. Yet it did sink, on its very first voyage, and about 1500 people drowned in the icy waters. The accident made headlines around the world.

The broken hull of the *Titanic*, as long as an 11-storey building, was lost for 75 years. The floor of the ocean was as remote as the planets in outer space. People wanted to visit the *Titanic*, but it rested in very deep water. At that depth, it is too dark, too cold, and the water pressure is too heavy for a diver wearing only a wetsuit and air tanks.

To solve the problem, scientists and engineers developed tiny submarines, called **submersibles**. These special craft can carry a few people far down into the ocean depths.

Pictures of the luxury ocean liner, the Titanic, were taken by aquanauts exploring the ship in tiny submarines called submersibles.

Today's Explorers

During the 1980s, a team of scientists began searching the ocean floor for the wreck of the *Titanic*. They used underwater radar and cameras to hunt for the vessel. In 1985 they found it about 650 km off the southeast coast of Newfoundland. Later they were able to visit the wreck in a submersible, glide along its rusted hull, collect artifacts with a robotic arm, and take pictures for everyone to see.

Over the years, people have discovered ways of travelling even deeper into the water. The chart below shows how far down into the ocean people can now explore. It also shows some of the creatures who make the deepest parts of the ocean their home.

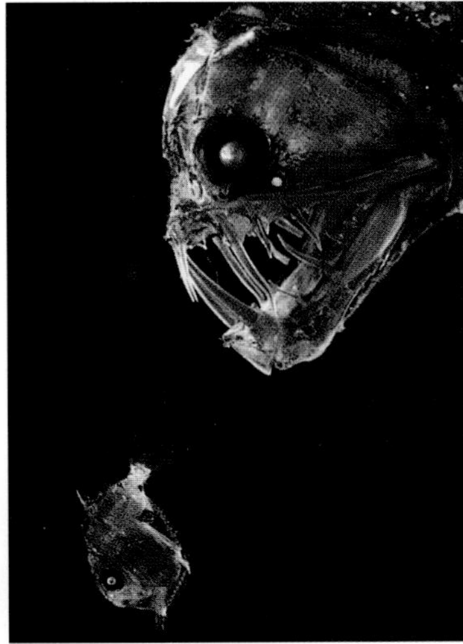

The deep-sea viperfish lures its prey into its cavernous mouth by dangling a glowing fin in front of its face.

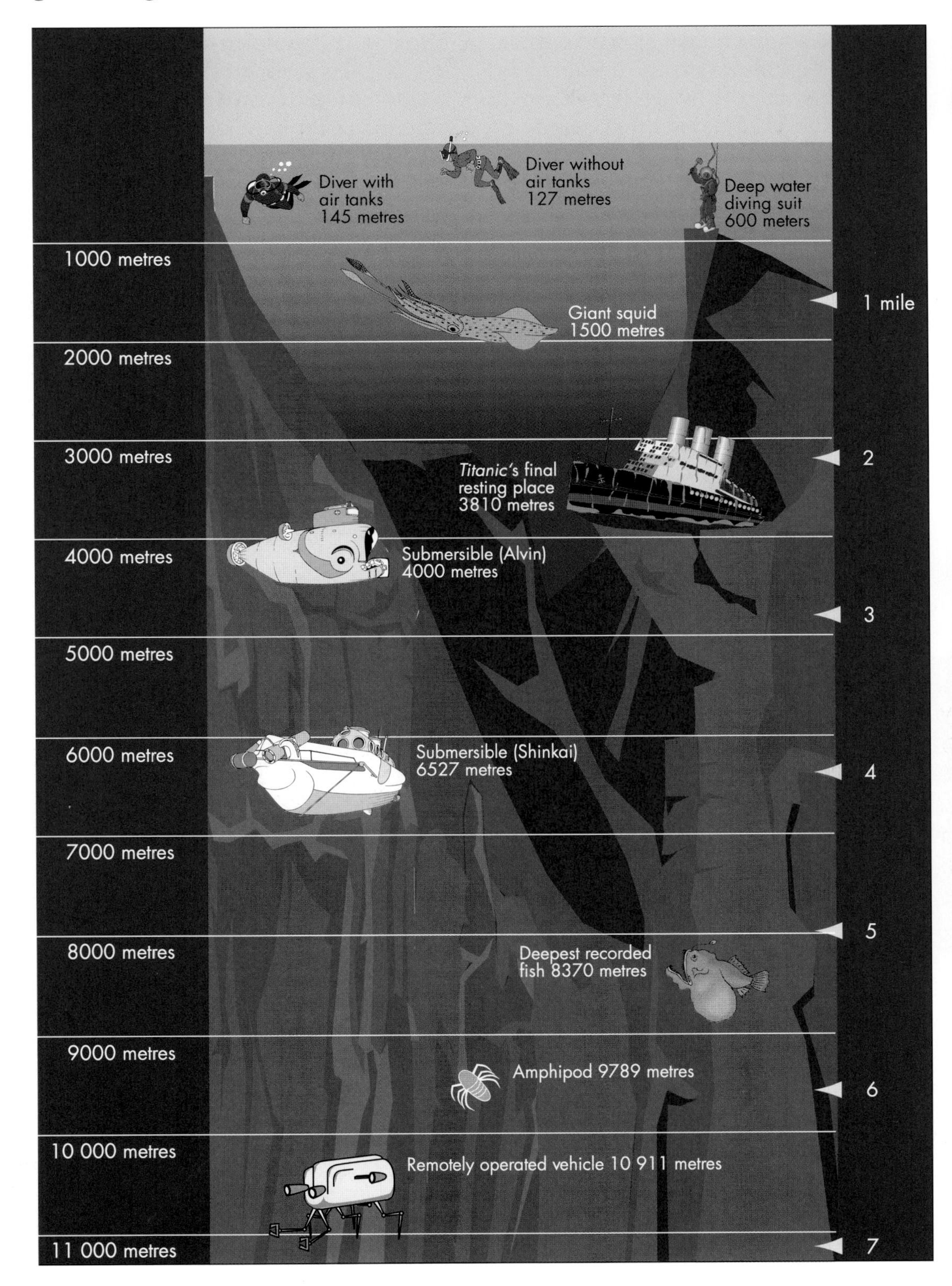

This anglerfish, also called the "common black devil," lives down deep in the ocean, under enormous water pressure. It may look menacing, but it grows to only about 13 cm in length.

27

Meanwhile, another set of explorers are active in the skies high above our planet. The exploration of space began in 1961 when a Russian **cosmonaut** named Yuri Gagarin rode a rocket in a single orbit around the Earth. The United States came close behind. After shooting several **astronauts** into space, the Americans landed the first person on the moon in 1969.

Canadians began to take part in space exploration in the 1980s. The first Canadian in space was Marc Garneau. He blasted off aboard the space shuttle *Challenger* in October 1984. (A shuttle is a space craft that can land back on Earth like an airplane.) Garneau has been followed by several others, including Roberta Bondar and Julie Payette, the first two Canadian women in space.

By the 1980s shuttle flights had become common. Each flight collected more and more information about the world above the Earth's atmosphere.

Life on board a space shuttle is a lot more comfortable than it was on the sailing ships of long ago, but it can still be a little topsy turvey. Astronauts do not feel the effects of gravity, the force that keeps us firmly planted on Earth. In space, where gravity is absent, objects don't weigh anything and float around in mid-air.

When they let go of their handholds, or unloosen their straps, astronauts float around the cabin of

Marc Garneau was the first Canadian to go into space. He spent eight days circling the Earth. In his baggage he carried the first hockey puck into space!

Julie Payette studied to be a computer engineer before she became an astronaut. She made her flight in 1999. She was the first Canadian to go aboard the ***space station*** *that the Russians built high above the Earth's surface.*

Roberta Bondar was the first Canadian woman in space. She is a medical doctor as well as an astronaut. She rode the shuttle Discovery in 1992.

the shuttle. When they are sleeping, they climb into sleeping bags that are strapped into the bunks. However, sometimes the astronauts prefer just to sleep while they float gently in the air.

What about eating? You may be surprised to learn that just like on the sailing ships of the past, explorers in shuttles do not have refrigerators. That means fruits and vegetables will stay fresh for only a few days. After that, the astronauts eat meals they would have eaten on Earth, except the foods have been dried so they will not spoil. The astronauts just add water to their food, and it is ready to eat! All food is served in special packages so that crumbs and leftovers do not fall into the equipment. Drinks come in special containers with straws attached. Remember, if the astronauts spill any water, it won't drop on the floor, but instead will drift off through the cabin until it splats into something, or someone!

Going to the washroom on a space shuttle is much the same as it is on Earth, except air is used to flush instead of water. Wastes and garbage are compressed and stored on the ship. Waste water is vented into space.

When they are shot into space, astronauts have to wear heavy suits with helmets. These weigh 35-45 kilograms each. Once they are in space, however, the astronauts wear everyday clothing. The shuttle is kept at a normal room temperature so the travellers are comfortable.

At the same time that astronauts are exploring space, many satellites without astronauts on board are making epic trips to distant planets. They send back images of deep space which tell us much about the universe in which we live.

One of Canada's greatest space inventions was the Canadarm. It has been part of the space shuttle program since the beginning. Canadarm is a long, remote-controlled arm that can lift and move heavy objects in space.

SOMETHING TO DO

1. What do humans gain from underwater exploration? Break up into small groups and brainstorm and record some answers to this question. Then, as a class choose the five most important things. Rate them from the most important to the least important.
2. Organize an exhibition called "Canadians in Space." Make posters describing the space shuttles and the space station. Find photographs of some Canadian astronauts. Build a model of the Canadarm. Information for your exhibition is available from the Canadian Space Agency in Ottawa. You can visit the Agency on the Internet at www.space.gc.ca.
3. Compare the challenges faced by astronauts with the challenges faced by early Canadian explorers. Make the comparison under different subject headings: transportation, clothing, food, dangers encountered. Who do you think faced the greater difficulties? Explain your answer.

28

he help offered by Aboriginal peoples was crucial to the success of the early explorers. In the same way, Aboriginal peoples continue to make important contributions to Canadian society today. There are about 800,000 First Nations, Inuit and Métis living in communities across Canada. They make important social, economic, and political contributions, whether as artists, lawyers, teachers, fishers, loggers, architects or community leaders.

ARTISTIC CONTRIBUTIONS

One of the many ways Aboriginal peoples have contributed to Canada is through their art. Art has always played an important role in Aboriginal society. The people used to decorate every item of their culture with designs and paintings. Masks, canoes, wooden bowls, woven baskets and totem poles are just some of the many objects we now think of as Aboriginal art.

Ojibwa artist Norval Morrisseau was one of the first modern Aboriginal artists in Ontario to appeal to a wide audience. Many of his paintings show Ojibwa legends and figures. This one is called Shaman and Disciples.

When Europeans arrived, they banned many of the Aboriginal ceremonies. They carried away the art objects to display in distant museums. The people themselves stopped making many of the items that had been a part of their culture for so many years. Aboriginal artists had to struggle to keep their traditions alive.

In the 1950s this trend began to reverse itself. On the West Coast, Aboriginal carvers began to make totem poles again. In the Arctic, Inuit began making soapstone carvings. In Ontario, artists began to paint the stories and legends of the First Nations. There has been a great revival of Aboriginal art since that time. Aboriginal people began to take a new pride in their traditions and wanted to share their cultures with others. In some places they demanded the return of objects that had been taken from them years earlier.

Inuit carvers create sculptures out of a soft rock called soapstone.

ABORIGINAL RIGHTS

There is a special relationship between the government of Canada and the Aboriginal peoples. Because they were the first inhabitants of the land, Aboriginal people have special rights, called **Aboriginal rights**. They have these rights because they were here first. The rights belong to Aboriginal people as

Aboriginal Peoples Today

Aboriginal people respect their traditional customs. One of these is the traditional gathering when people come together to take part in dancing, feasting, and other activities. Traditional gatherings are called by different names in different parts of Canada. Whatever they are called, they are an important social and ceremonial occasion for Aboriginal people.

a group and are part of the Constitution of Canada.

The special relationship between the government and the Aboriginal people is spelled out in the Indian Act. The Indian Act is a law passed by the government in 1876. (It was called the Indian Act because, at the time, Aboriginal people were called Indians.) The Indian Act outlined what Aboriginal people could and could not do. Among many other things, it said how the people could choose their leaders, when they could travel outside their communities, and what customs they were allowed to continue. The Indian Act is carried out by the Department of Indian Affairs, a branch of the federal government. The details of the law have changed over the years, but it remains in place.

The Indian Act gave the government control over almost every aspect of the lives of Aboriginal people. The Indian Act even said who was an Aboriginal person and who was not. It was used to take away some of the rights that other Canadians had. For example, it was used to ban some Aboriginal religious customs, and until 1960 Aboriginal people were not allowed to vote in elections like other Canadians.

TREATIES AND LAND CLAIMS

Treaties are a part of the special relationship between Aboriginal people and the government. **Treaties** are written agreements that have been made between the Aboriginal groups and the government. Treaties were made as early as the 1700s between the British colonists and the Aboriginal people. Sometimes these were friendship treaties promising peace and goodwill. Sometimes they were treaties of alliance in warfare. In Ontario the various Aboriginal groups agreed to share their land in return for annual payments of money and goods.

Between 1871 and 1921 a series of 11 treaties were made in western and northern Canada. According to these treaties, Aboriginal peoples agreed to share their traditional lands. On the other hand, the government agreed to:

- make cash payments to the Aboriginal groups
- set aside small areas of land, called reserves, for the use of Aboriginal groups
- permit the Aboriginal peoples to hunt and fish as they have always done.

DID YOU KNOW?

Today in Canada many Aboriginal people live on reserves. There are about 2300 reserves across Canada. About one out of every three Aboriginal people lives on a reserve.

Aboriginal people have special respect for their Elders. They believe that life experience has given the Elders special wisdom. Elders help the children to learn about traditional knowledge and history. They also take part in community decision making.

The government signed the treaties because it wanted the land for settlement and railway building. The Aboriginal people agreed because their way of life was changing and they hoped the treaties would help them adjust to the changes.

Many years passed without any new treaties being made. Then in 1975, the Cree people in Northern Quebec signed an agreement that allowed much of their hunting lands to be flooded by a new power dam. In 1999, the Nisga'a people in northern British Columbia also signed a treaty, the first one in that province in a hundred years.

Treaty making is an ongoing process. Treaties recognize that Aboriginal people have rights to their land. These rights are called **land claims**. Treaties are a way of settling the claims in a way that is fair to both sides.

ABORIGINAL SELF-GOVERNMENT

Aboriginal peoples see no reason why they should have to give up their lands and their cultures in order to be part of Canada. They want to keep their languages and their own way of life, while remaining members of Canadian society. They want to make their own decisions about things that will affect their lives. They call this **self-government**. They will still be part of Canada, but it means that they will be able to have more control over their affairs.

A kind of self-government already exists in many Aboriginal communities. Many communities are like local governments. They run their own schools and health services. For example, in the territory of Nunavut, created in 1999, Inuit people are the majority and control the government.

Aboriginal peoples say that self-government is not something that they want the government to give them. They say that it is a right that they already have. They just want other Canadians to recognize it.

Along with self-government, there are many social and economic issues facing Aboriginal people. Because they have not received the same opportunities as other Canadians, Aboriginal people are not as well off as non-Aboriginals. They have more trouble getting a good education and finding jobs. In some Aboriginal communities, houses are in poor condition and sickness is common.

Aboriginal people are working to overcome these disadvantages, sometimes on their own, sometimes with the help of government. More and more Aboriginal people are going to university, starting successful businesses and joining the workforce in many walks of life. At the same time, they are also finding strength in their traditions and beliefs.

Self-government is part of this process. There are many questions still to be answered about self-government. It may take different forms in different parts of the country. What is important is that Aboriginal people today are taking more control over their own lives.